BIBLE PROMISES
FOR SUPERNATURAL LIVING

Alice Chapin was born in Batavia, New York. She has worked as a radio newswriter, newspaper reporter and columnist, free lance feature writer and elementary school teacher. Her articles appear in many periodicals. She lives in Newnan, Georgia with her husband, Norman, and both are on the staff of Campus Crusade for Christ International. Mrs. Chapin is also tht author of 500 CREATIVE WAYS TO SAY "I LOVE YOU," a woman's marriage guide.

BIBLE PROMISES
FOR
SUPERNATURAL
LIVING

Compiled by Alice Chapin

HERE'S LIFE PUBLISHERS, INC.
San Bernardino, California 92402

BIBLE PROMISES FOR SUPERNATURAL LIVING

Compiled by Alice Chapin

A Campus Crusade for Christ Book

Published by
HERE'S LIFE PUBLISHERS, INC.
P.O. Box 1576, San Bernardino, CA 92402

Fifth Printing, 1985

ISBN 0-86605-101-5
HLP Product No. 400481

Manufactured in the United States of America

FOR MORE INFORMATION, WRITE:

L.I.F.E.—P. O. Box A399, Sydney South 2000, Australia
Campus Crusade for Christ of Canada—Box 368, Abbottsford, B.C., V25 4N9, Canada
Campus Crusade for Christ—103 Friar Street, Reading RGI IEP, Berkshire, England
Campus Crusade for Christ—28 Westmoreland St., Dublin 2, Ireland
Lay Institute for Evangelism—P. O. Box 8786, Auckland 3, New Zealand
Life Ministry—P. O. Box/Bus 91015, Auckland Park 2006, Republic of So. Africa
Campus Crusade for Christ Int'l.—Arrowhead Springs, San Bernardino, CA 92414, U.S.A.

*To my parents, William and Viola Zillman,
who bothered to bring me up decently.
Thanks to them, when the gospel was
introduced to me, I was ready.*

The whole Bible was given us by inspiration from God and is useful to teach us what is true and to make us realize what is wrong in our lives; it straightens us out and helps us do what is right. It is God's way of making us well prepared at every point, fully equipped to do good to everyone.

2 Timothy 3:16, 17

But when I am afraid, I will put my confidence in You. Yes, I will trust the promises of God. And since I am trusting Him, what can mere man do to me?

Psalm 56:3, 4

CONTENTS

A WORD FROM THE EDITOR:

For years, it seemed I spent too many hours attempting to locate just the right Scripture verses for coping with daily problems. Sometimes, I would waken in the middle of the night seeking consolation, advice or guidance. But the healing verses were so elusive! I knew the valuable help was there in the Bible, but where? Wherever could I look for answers if I felt afraid, sad, angry or lonely? Surely, it should not be necessary to consult a busy clergyman to find some uplifting reading in God's Word that would apply to specific situations.

That is why I compiled BIBLE PROMISES FOR SUPERNATURAL LIVING. It is a self-help book made to be worn out by daily use. Those elusive portions of Scripture have been preselected and printed in their entirety on these pages for easy fingertip reference. No more thumbing through all 66 books of the Bible to locate appropriate words or promises to match your problem, mend your attitude, renew your mind, or simply praise God on happy days. Just open to the chapter that suits your mood and there they are. And you can easily return to these verses again and again.

Fellow Christian, boldly and strongly affirm these positive Scripture promises! Read them aloud! Memorize them! Constantly and deliberately act on them as absolute truth! They are the keys to a supernaturally satisfying life even in this harried, hurried, and hectic 20th century.

To the reader who is still a "searcher of truth": if you have not yet committed your life to Christ, turn to the back pages of this book to find out how to establish a "born anew" relationship with the God of the Universe, so you too can apply Bible promises.

Alice Chapin
Newnan, Georgia 30265

WHO IS THIS GOD?
DOES HE WORK IN
YOUR BEHALF?
IS HE BIG ENOUGH?

Isaiah 40

18 How can we describe God? With what can we compare Him?

22 It is God who sits above the circle of the earth. (The people below must seem to Him like grasshoppers!) He is the one who stretches out the heavens like a curtain and makes His tent from them.

23 He dooms the great men of the world and brings them all to naught.

24 They hardly get started, barely take root, when He blows on them and their work withers and the wind carries them off like straw.

25 "With whom will you compare Me? Who is My equal?" asks the Holy One.

26 Look up into the heavens! Who created all these stars? As a shepherd leads his sheep, calling each by its pet name, and counts them to see that none are lost or strayed, so God does with stars and planets!

Amos 4

12b ...Meet your God...

13 For you are dealing with the one who formed the mountains and made the winds, and knows your every thought; He turns the morning to darkness and crushes down the mountains underneath His feet: Jehovah, the Lord, the God of Hosts, is His name.

Psalm 107

23 And then there are the sailors sailing the seven seas, plying the trade routes of the world.

24 They, too, observe the power of God in action.

25 He calls to the storm winds; the waves rise high.

26 Their ships are tossed to the heavens and sink again to the depths; the sailors cringe in terror.

27 They reel and stagger like drunkards and are at their wit's end.

28 Then they cry to the Lord in their trouble, and He saves them.

29 He calms the storm and stills the waves.

30 What a blessing is that stillness, as He brings them safely into harbor!

31 Oh, that these men would praise the Lord for His lovingkindness and for all of His wonderful deeds!

1

When You Feel AFRAID, ANXIOUS, WORRIED

MIND RENEWAL PROMISE:
Romans 8

31 What can we ever say to such wonderful things as these? If God is on our side, who can ever be against us?

WHY WORRY?
Matthew 6

25 So my counsel is: Don't worry about *things*—food, drink, and clothes. For you already have life and a body—and they are far more important than what to eat and wear.

28 And why worry about your clothes? Look at the field lilies! They don't worry about theirs.

29 Yet King Solomon in all his glory was not clothed as beautifully as they.

30 And if God cares so wonderfully for flowers that are here today and gone tomorrow, won't He more surely care for you, O men of little faith?

26 Look at the birds! They don't worry about what to eat—they don't need to sow or reap or store up food—for your heavenly Father feeds them. And you are far more valuable to Him than they are.

Luke 12

25 And besides, what's the use of worrying? What good does it do? Will it add a single day to your life? Of course not!

GOD DIRECTS YOUR STEPS
Proverbs 20

24 Since the Lord is directing our steps, why try to understand everything that happens along the way?

HOW TO STOP WORRYING
Philippians 4

4 Always be full of joy in the Lord; I say it again, rejoice!

6 Don't worry about anything; instead, pray about everything; tell God your needs and don't forget to thank Him for His answers.

ONE DAY AT A TIME
Matthew 6

34 So don't be anxious about tomorrow. God will take care of your tomorrow too. Live one day at a time.

GOD CARRIES BURDENS
Psalm 55

17 I will pray morning, noon, and night, pleading aloud with God; and He will hear and answer.

18 Though the tide of battle runs strongly against me, for so many are fighting me, yet He will rescue me.

22 Give your burdens to the Lord. He will carry them. He will not permit the godly to slip or fall.

PUT GOD FIRST, THEN EXPECT SUCCESS
Proverbs 3

6 In everything you do, put God first, and He will direct you and crown your efforts with success.

Luke 12

30 All mankind scratches for its daily bread, but your heavenly Father knows your needs.

31 He will always give you all you need from day to day if you will make the Kingdom of God your primary concern.

GOD KNOWS YOUR NEEDS
Matthew 6

31,32 So don't worry at all about having enough food and clothing. Why be like the heathen? For they take pride in all these things and are deeply concerned about them. But your heavenly Father already knows perfectly well that you need them,

33 And He will give them to you if you give Him first place in your life.

IF GOD IS FOR YOU, WHO CAN BE AGAINST YOU?
Psalm 56

8 You have seen me tossing and turning through the night. You have collected all my tears and preserved them in Your bottle! You have recorded every one in Your book.

9 The very day I call for help, the tide of battle turns. My enemies flee! This one thing I *know: God is for me!*

THE LORD IS ON MY SIDE
Psalm 118

1 Oh, thank the Lord, for He's so good! His lovingkindness is forever.

5 In my distress I prayed to the Lord and He answered me and rescued me.

6 He is for me! How can I be afraid? What can mere man do to me?

7 The Lord is on my side, He will help me. Let those who hate me beware.

8 It is better to trust the Lord than to put confidence in men.

9 It is better to take refuge in Him than in the mightiest king!

THE STEADYING EFFECT OF TRUST
Psalm 125

1 Those who trust in the Lord are steady as Mount Zion, unmoved by any circumstance.

2 Just as the mountains surround and protect Jerusalem, so the Lord surrounds and protects His people.

A STRONG FOUNDATION
Luke 6

47,48 But all those who come and listen and obey Me are like a man who builds a house on a strong foundation laid upon the underlying rock. When the floodwaters rise and break against the house, it stands firm, for it is strongly built.

MESSAGE FROM GOD:
TO THE ANXIOUS...
Isaiah 41

10 Fear not, for I am with you. Do not be dismayed. I am your God. I will strengthen you; I will help you; I will uphold you with My victorious right hand.

13 I am holding you by your right hand—I, the Lord your God—and I say to you, Don't be afraid; I am here to help you.

I AM WITH YOU
Jeremiah 1

17 Get up and dress and go out and tell them whatever I tell you to say. Don't be afraid of them, or else I will make a fool of you in front of them.

18 For see, today I have made you impervious to their attacks. They cannot harm you. You are strong like a fortified city that cannot be captured, like an iron pillar and heavy gates of brass. All the kings of Judah and its officers and priests and people will not be able to prevail against you.

19 "They will try, but they will fail. For I am with you," says the Lord. "I will deliver you."

THIS IS THE KIND OF GOD
YOU HAVE AVAILABLE FOR HELP
Mark 4

35 As evening fell, Jesus said to his disciples, "Let's cross to the other side of the lake."

36 So they took Him just as He was and started out, leaving the crowds behind (though other boats followed).

37 But soon a terrible storm arose. High waves

began to break into the boat until it was nearly full of water and about to sink.

38 Jesus was asleep at the back of the boat with His head on a cushion. Frantically they wakened Him, shouting, "Teacher, don't You even care that we are all about to drown?"

39 Then He rebuked the wind and said to the sea, "Quiet down!" And the wind fell, and there was a great calm!

40 And He asked them, "Why were you so fearful? Don't you even yet have confidence in Me?"

41 And they were filled with awe and said among themselves, "Who is this man that even the winds and seas obey Him?"

JESUS: YESTERDAY, TODAY, FOREVER
Hebrews 13

6b ...We can say without any doubt or fear, "The Lord is my Helper and I am not afraid of anything that mere man can do to me."

8 Jesus Christ is the same yesterday, today, and forever.

AFFIRM GOD'S HELP
(Why not read this aloud?)
Psalm 18

32 He fills me with strength and protects me wherever I go.

33 He gives me the surefootedness of a mountain goat upon the crags. He leads me safely along the top of the cliffs.

35 You have given me Your salvation as my shield. Your right hand, O Lord, supports me; Your gentleness has made me great.

36 You have made wide steps beneath my feet so that I need never slip.

SCRIPTURE FOR A PEACEFUL MINDSET
Psalm 121

1 Shall I look to the mountain gods for help?

2 No! My help is from Jehovah who made the mountains! And the heavens too!

3,4 He will never let me stumble, slip or fall. For He is always watching, never sleeping.

5 Jehovah Himself is caring for you! He is your defender.

6 He protects you day and night.

THE LORD, MY SHEPHERD
Psalm 23

1 Because the Lord is my Shepherd, I have everything I need!

2,3 He lets me rest in the meadow grass and leads me beside the quiet streams. He restores my failing health. He helps me do what honors Him the most.

4 Even when walking through the dark valley of death I will not be afraid, for You are close beside me, guarding, guiding all the way.

5 You provide delicious food for me in the presence of my enemies. You have welcomed me as Your guest; blessings overflow!

6 Your goodness and unfailing kindness shall be with me all of my life, and afterwards I will live with You forever in Your home.

THOUGH A MIGHTY ARMY
MARCHES AGAINST ME
Psalm 27

1 The Lord is my light and my salvation; whom shall I fear?

2 When evil men come to destroy me, they will stumble and fall!

3 Yes, though a mighty army marches against me, my heart shall know no fear! I am confident that God will save me.

13 I am expecting the Lord to rescue me again, so that once again I will see His goodness to me here in the land of the living.

14 Don't be impatient. Wait for the Lord, and He will come and save you! Be brave, stout-hearted and courageous. Yes, wait and He will help you.

A PLACE OF SAFETY
Psalm 59

9 O God my Strength! I will sing Your praises, for You are my place of safety.

10 My God is changeless in His love for me and He will come and help me...

16 ...I will sing each morning about Your power and mercy. For You have been my high tower of refuge, a place of safety in the day of my distress.

17 O my Strength, to You I sing my praises; for You are my high tower of safety, my God of mercy.

2

When You Are ALONE, LONESOME

MIND RENEWAL PROMISE:
Psalm 139

7 I can *never* be lost to Your Spirit! I can *never* get away from my God!

8 If I go up to heaven, You are there; if I go down to the place of the dead, You are there.

9 If I ride the morning winds to the farthest oceans,

10 Even there Your hand will guide me, Your strength will support me.

GOD IS CLOSE BY
Psalm 145

14 The Lord lifts the fallen and those bent beneath their loads.

18 He is close to all who call on Him sincerely.

Joshua 1

9 Yes, be bold and strong! Banish fear and doubt! For remember, the Lord your God is with you wherever you go.

YOU HAVE A "BEST" FRIEND
Psalm 54

4 But God is my helper. He is a friend of mine!

Psalm 14

5b ...For God is with those who love Him.

WELCOME
Ephesians 3

12 Now we can come fearlessly right into God's presence, assured of His glad welcome when we come with Christ and trust in Him.

NEVER, NEVER FORGOTTEN
Isaiah 49

14 They say, "My Lord deserted us; He has forgotten us."

15 Never! Can a mother forget her little child and not have love for her own son? Yet even if that should be, I will not forget you.

YOU HAVE A FAMILY
1 Peter 1

2 Dear friends, God the Father chose you long ago and knew you would become His children.

Ephesians 1

4 Long ago, even before He made the world, God chose us to be His very own, through what Christ would do for us; He decided then to make us holy in His eyes, without a single fault—we who stand before Him covered with His love.

5 His unchanging plan has always been to adopt us into His own family by sending Jesus Christ to die for us. And He did this because He wanted to!

BROTHER (OR SISTER) OF JESUS
Hebrews 2

11 We who have been made holy by Jesus, now have the same Father He has. That is why Jesus is not ashamed to call us His brothers.

12 For He says in the book of Psalms, "I will talk to My brothers about God My Father, and together we will sing His praises."

YOU HAVE THE HOLY SPIRIT
John 14

15,16 If you love Me, obey Me; and I will ask the Father and He will give you another Comforter, and He will never leave you.

17 He is the Holy Spirit, the Spirit who leads into all truth. The world at large cannot receive Him, for it isn't looking for Him and doesn't recognize Him. But you do, for He lives with you now and some day shall be in you.

18 No, I will not abandon you or leave you as orphans in the storm—I will come to you.

YOU HAVE A COUNTRY
AND FELLOW CITIZENS
Ephesians 2

12b ...You were lost, without God, without hope.

13 But now you belong to Christ Jesus, and though you once were far away from God, now you have been brought very near to Him because of what Jesus Christ has done for you with His blood.

18 Now all of us, whether Jews or Gentiles, may come to God the Father with the Holy Spirit's help because of what Christ has done for us.

19 Now you are no longer strangers to God and foreigners to heaven, but you are members of God's very own family, citizens of God's country, and you belong in God's household with every other Christian.

21 We who believe are carefully joined together with Christ as parts of a beautiful, constantly growing temple for God.

22 And you also are joined with Him and with each other by the Spirit, and are part of this dwelling place of God.

YOU ARE LOVED INCREDIBLY
Romans 8

35 Who then can ever keep Christ's love from us? When we have trouble or calamity, when we are hunted down or destroyed, is it because He doesn't love us anymore? And if we are hungry, or penniless, or in danger, or threatened with death, has God deserted us?

38 ...I am convinced that nothing can ever separate us from His love. Death can't, and life can't. The angels won't, and all the powers of hell itself cannot keep God's love away. Our fears for today, our worries about tomorrow,

39 Or where we are—high above the sky, or in the deepest ocean—nothing will ever be able to separate us from the love of God demonstrated by our Lord Jesus Christ when He died for us.

James 1

9 A Christian who doesn't amount to much in this world should be glad, for he is great in the Lord's sight.

GOD EVEN KNOWS WHEN
YOU SIT OR STAND
Psalm 139

1 O Lord, You have examined my heart and know everything about me.

2 You know when I sit or stand. When far away You know my every thought.

3 You chart the path ahead of me, and tell me where to stop and rest. Every moment, You know where I am.

4 You know what I am going to say before I even say it.

CONSTANTLY AWARE OF YOU
Hebrews 4

13 He knows about everyone, everywhere. Everything about us is bare and wide open to the all-seeing eyes of our living God.

CONSTANTLY WATCHING
YOUR PROGRESS
Psalm 32

8 I will instruct you (says the Lord) and guide you along the best pathway for your life; I will advise you and watch your progress.

CONSTANTLY THINKING
ABOUT YOU
1 Peter 5

7 Let Him have all your worries and cares, for He is always thinking about you and watching everything that concerns you.

GOD CONSTANTLY
SURROUNDS YOU
Psalm 32

7 You are my hiding place from every storm of life; You even keep me from getting into trouble! You surround me with songs of victory.

Psalm 91

1 We live within the shadow of the Almighty, sheltered by the God who is above all gods.

2 This I declare, that He alone is my refuge, my place of safety; He is my God, and I am trusting Him.

MY FRIEND GOD
....HOW GREAT HE IS!!
Proverbs 30

4 Who else but God goes back and forth to heaven? Who else holds the wind in His fists, and wraps up the oceans in His cloak? Who but God has created the world? If there is any other, what is his name and his son's name—if you know it?

Isaiah 48

12 Listen to Me, My people, My chosen ones! I alone am God. I am the First; I am the Last.

13 It was My hand that laid the foundations of the earth; the palm of My right hand spread out the heavens above; I spoke and they came into being.

3

When You Feel DEPRESSED, DISCOURAGED, FRUSTRATED

MIND RENEWAL PROMISE:
Isaiah 43

2 When you go through deep waters and great trouble, I will be with you. When you go through rivers of difficulty, you will not drown! When you walk through the fire of oppression, you will not be burned up—the flames will not consume you.

YOU ARE NOT THE ONLY ONE FEELING DOWN
1 Peter 5

7 Let Him have all your worries and cares, for He is always thinking about you and watching everything that concerns you.

8 Be careful—watch out for attacks from Satan, your great enemy. He prowls around like a hungry, roaring lion, looking for some victim to tear apart.

9 Stand firm when he attacks. Trust the Lord; and remember that other Christians all around the world are going through these sufferings too.

OTHERS HAVE FELT THE SAME WAY
Psalm 31

9,10 O Lord, have mercy on me in my anguish. My eyes are red from weeping; my health is broken from sorrow. I am pining away with grief; my years are shortened, drained away because of sadness. My sins have sapped my strength; I stoop with sorrow and with shame.

12 I am forgotten like a dead man, like a broken and discarded pot.

THERE MAY BE A PURPOSE
IN YOUR FRUSTRATION
Isaiah 30

18 Yet the Lord still waits for you to come to Him, so He can show you His love; He will conquer you to bless you, just as He said. For the Lord is faithful to His promises. Blessed are all those who wait for Him to help them.

1 Peter 1

6 So be truly glad! There is wonderful joy ahead, even though the going is rough for a while down here.

7 These trials are only to test your faith, to see whether or not it is strong and pure. It is being tested as fire tests gold and purifies it—and your faith is far more precious to God than mere gold; so if your faith remains strong after being tried in the test tube of fiery trials, it will bring you much praise and glory and honor on the day of His return.

THE GREATER YOUR SUFFERING, THE GREATER GOD'S COMFORT
2 Corinthians 1

3,4 What a wonderful God we have—He is the Father of our Lord Jesus Christ, the source of every mercy, and the one who so wonderfully comforts and strengthens us in our hardships and trials. And why does He do this? So that when others are troubled, needing our sympathy and encouragement, we can pass on to them this same help and comfort God has given us.

5 You can be sure that the more we undergo sufferings for Christ, the more He will shower us with His comfort and encouragement.

GOD IS WITH YOU EVEN THOUGH YOU *FEEL* OTHERWISE
Psalm 40

17 I am poor and needy, yet the Lord is thinking about me right now! O my God, You are my helper. You are my Savior.

HELD IN HIS HAND
Psalm 37

23 The steps of good men are directed by the Lord. He delights in each step they take.

24 If they fall it isn't fatal, for the Lord holds them with His hand.

NEVER FORSAKEN
Hebrews 13

5b ...For God has said, "I will never, *never* fail you nor forsake you."

6 That is why we can say without any doubt or fear, "The Lord is my Helper and I am not afraid of anything that mere man can do to me."

ANGELS TO STEADY YOU

Psalm 91

1 We live within the shadow of the Almighty, sheltered by the God who is above all gods.

2 This I declare, that He alone is my refuge, my place of safety; He is my God, and I am trusting Him.

3 For He rescues you from every trap, and protects you from the fatal plague.

4 He will shield you with His wings! They will shelter you. His faithful promises are your armor.

5 Now you don't need to be afraid of the dark any more, nor fear the dangers of the day;

6 Nor dread the plagues of darkness, nor disasters in the morning.

7 Though a thousand fall at my side, though ten thousand are dying around me, the evil will not touch me.

8 I will see how the wicked are punished but I will not share it.

9 For Jehovah is my refuge! I choose the God above all gods to shelter me.

10 How then can evil overtake me or any plague come near?

11 For He orders his angels to protect you wherever you go.

12 They will steady you with their hands to keep you from stumbling against the rocks on the trail.

GOD HAS AUTHORITY OVER
EVERY PART OF YOUR LIFE
Colossians 2

6 And now just as you trusted Christ to save you, trust Him, too, for each day's problems; live in vital union with Him.

7 Let your roots grow down into Him and draw up nourishment from Him. See that you go on growing in the Lord, and become strong and vigorous in the truth you were taught. Let your lives overflow with joy and thanksgiving for all He has done.

8 Don't let others spoil your faith and joy with their philosophies, their wrong and shallow answers built on men's thoughts and ideas, instead of on what Christ has said.

9 For in Christ there is all of God in a human body;

10 *So you have everything when you have Christ*, and you are filled with God through your union with Christ. He is the highest Ruler, with authority over every other power.

INCREDIBLE HELPING POWER
Deuteronomy 33

26 There is none like the God of Jerusalem—
   He descends from the heavens
   In majestic splendor to help you.

27 The eternal God is your Refuge,
   And underneath are the everlasting arms.

GOD HEARS YOUR CRIES FOR HELP
Psalm 40

1 I waited patiently for God to help me; then He listened and heard my cry.

2 He lifted me out of the pit of despair, out from the bog and the mire, and set my feet on a hard, firm path and steadied me as I walked along.

3 He has given me a new song to sing, of praises to our God. Now many will hear of the glorious things He did for me, and stand in awe before the Lord, and put their trust in Him.

4 Many blessings are given to those who trust the Lord, and have no confidence in those who are proud, or who trust in idols.

PRAY LIKE THIS:
Psalm 61

1 O God, listen to me! Hear my prayer!

2 For wherever I am, though far away at the ends of the earth, I will cry to You for help. When my heart is faint and overwhelmed, lead me to the mighty, towering Rock of safety.

3 For You are my refuge, a high tower where my enemies can never reach me.

HOPE
1 Peter 5

10 After you have suffered a little while, our God, who is full of kindness through Christ, will give you His eternal glory. He personally will come and pick you up, and set you firmly in place, and make you stronger than ever.

11 To Him be all power over all things, forever and ever. Amen.

LOVINGKINDNESS FRESH EACH DAY
Lamentations 3

17 O Lord, all peace and all prosperity have long since gone, for You have taken them away. I have forgotten what enjoyment is.

18 All hope is gone; my strength has turned to water, for the Lord has left me.

21 *Yet there is one ray of hope:*

22 *His compassion never ends.* It is only the Lord's mercies that have kept us from complete destruction.

23 Great is His faithfulness; His lovingkindness begins afresh each day.

CURES FOR DEPRESSION:

Praise: (it will lift your spirits)
Psalm 34

1 I will praise the Lord no matter what happens. I will constantly speak of His glories and grace.

2 I will boast of all His kindness to me. Let all who are discouraged take heart.

3 Let us praise the Lord together, and exalt His name.

Pray: (it will give you peace)
Philippians 4

6 Don't worry about anything; instead, pray about everything; tell God your needs and don't forget to thank Him for His answers.

7 If you do this you will experience God's peace, which is far more wonderful than the human mind can understand. His peace will keep your thoughts and your hearts quiet and at rest as you trust in Christ Jesus.

Realize this!
Romans 8

26 And in the same way—by our faith—the Holy Spirit helps us with our daily problems and in our praying. For we don't even know what we

should pray for, nor how to pray as we should; but the Holy Spirit prays for us with such feeling that it cannot be expressed in words.

Trust God:
Proverbs 3

7,8 Don't be conceited, sure of your own wisdom. Instead, trust and reverence the Lord, and turn your back on evil; when you do that, then you will be given renewed health and vitality.

Think positive thoughts:
Philippians 4

8 And now, brothers, as I close this letter let me say this one more thing: Fix your thoughts on what is true and good and right. Think about things that are pure and lovely, and dwell on the fine, good things in others. Think about all you can praise God for and be glad about.

Give thanks:
Psalm 107

1 Say "Thank You" to the Lord for being so loving and kind.
2 Has the Lord redeemed you? Then speak out! Tell others He has saved you from your enemies.
43 Listen, if you are wise, to what I am saying. Think about the lovingkindness of the Lord!

Get rid of griping:
Proverbs 15

4 Gentle words cause life and health; griping brings discouragement.

See yourself as God sees you:
2 Corinthians 2

15 As far as God is concerned there is a sweet, wholesome fragrance in our lives. It is the fragrance of Christ within us, an aroma to both the saved and the unsaved all around us.

16 To those who are not being saved, we seem a fearful smell of death and doom, while to those who know Christ we are a life-giving perfume.

Claim God's power:
Ephesians 3

20 Now glory be to God who by His mighty power at work within us is able to do far more than we would ever dare to ask or even dream of—infinitely beyond our highest prayers, desires, thoughts, or hopes.

Don't look back!
Philippians 3

13 No, dear brothers, I am still not all I should be but I am bringing all my energies to bear on this one thing: Forgetting the past and looking forward to what lies ahead,

14 I strain to reach the end of the race and receive the prize for which God is calling us up to heaven because of what Christ Jesus did for us.

POWER PROMISE FROM JESUS
Matthew 11

28 Come to Me and I will give you rest—all of you who work so hard beneath a heavy yoke.

29,30 Wear My yoke—for it fits perfectly—and let Me teach you; for I am gentle and humble, and you shall find rest for your souls; for I give you only light burdens.

POWERFUL THOUGHT
Psalm 103

13 He is like a father to us, tender and sympathetic to those who reverence Him.

14 For He knows we are but dust,

15 And that our days are few and brief, like grass, like flowers,

16 Blown by the wind and gone forever.

17,18 But the lovingkindness of the Lord is from everlasting to everlasting, to those who reverence Him.

4

When You Feel
GOD IS FAR AWAY

MIND RENEWAL PROMISE:
Acts 2

25b ...I know the Lord is always with me. He is helping me. God's mighty power supports me.

GOD PROMISED...
"THOSE WHO SEEK ME WILL FIND ME"
Acts 17

25 He Himself gives life and breath to everything, and satisfies every need there is.

27 His purpose in all of this is that they should seek after God, and perhaps feel their way toward Him and find Him—though He is not far from any one of us.

28 For in Him we live and move and are!...We are the sons of God.

THERE IS ONLY ONE THING THAT
SEPARATES A PERSON FROM GOD—SIN
James 4

4 Don't you realize that making friends with God's enemies—the evil pleasures of this world—makes you an enemy of God? I say it again, that if your aim is to enjoy the evil pleasure of the unsaved world, you cannot also be a friend of God.

CONFESSION HEALS SEPARATION
James 4

7 ....Resist the devil and he will flee from you.

8 And when you draw close to God, God will draw close to you. Wash your hands, you sinners, and let your hearts be filled with God alone to make them pure and true to Him.

THE DOOR IS OPEN
Revelation 3

20 Look! I have been standing at the door and I am constantly knocking. If anyone hears Me calling him and opens the door, I will come in and fellowship with him and he with Me.

THE HEALING PRAYER
Psalm 139

23 Search me, O God, and know my heart; test my thoughts.

24 Point out anything You find in me that makes You sad, and lead me along the path of everlasting life.

THE BREACH HEALED—DRAW NEAR
Hebrews 7

19b ...For Christ makes us acceptable to God, and now we may draw near to Him.

Psalm 66

8 Let everyone bless God and sing His praises,

9 For He holds our lives in His hands! And He holds our feet to the path!

16 Come and hear, all of you who reverence the Lord, and I will tell you what He did for me:

17 For I cried to Him for help, with praises ready on my tongue.

18 He would not have listened if I had not confessed my sins.

19 But He listened! He heard my prayer! He paid attention to it!

20 Blessed be God who didn't turn away when I was praying, and didn't refuse me His kindness and love.

NOTHING BETWEEN
Colossians 1

20 It was through what His Son did that God cleared a path for everything to come to Him—all things in heaven and on earth—for Christ's death on the cross has made peace with God for all by His blood.

21 This includes you who were once so far away from God. You were His enemies and hated Him and were separated from Him by your evil thoughts and actions, yet now He has brought you back as His friends.

22 He has done this through the death on the cross of His own human body, and now as a result Christ has brought you into the very presence of God, and you are standing there before Him with nothing left against you—nothing left that He could even chide you for.

23 The only condition is that you fully believe the Truth, standing in it steadfast and firm, strong in the Lord, convinced of the Good News that Jesus died for you, and never shifting from trusting Him to save you.

A CLEAR PATH
Hebrews 10

19 And so, dear brothers, now we may walk right into the very Holy of Holies where God is, because of the blood of Jesus.

20 This is the fresh, new, life-giving way which Christ has opened up for us by tearing the curtain—His human body—to let us into the holy presence of God.

21 And since this great High Priest of ours rules over God's household,

22 Let us go right in, to God Himself, with true hearts fully trusting Him to receive us, because we have been sprinkled with Christ's blood to make us clean, and because our bodies have been washed with the pure water.

DON'T TRUST YOUR FEELINGS ...CLAIM THE TRUTH!
2 Corinthians 1

22 He has put His brand upon us—His mark of ownership—and given us His Holy Spirit in our hearts as guarantee that we belong to Him, and as the first installment of all that He is going to give us.

GOD KNOWS WHERE YOU ARE EVERY MOMENT
Psalm 139

7 I can *never* be lost to Your Spirit! I can *never* get away from my God!

11 If I try to hide in the darkness, the night becomes light around me.

12 For even darkness cannot hide from God; to You the night shines as bright as day. Darkness and light are both alike to You.

17,18 How precious it is, Lord, to realize that You are thinking about me constantly! I can't even count how many times a day Your thoughts turn towards me. And when I waken in the morning, You are still thinking of me!

GOD NEVER SLEEPS
Psalm 121

3,4 He will never let me stumble, slip or fall. For He is always watching, never sleeping.

5 Jehovah Himself is caring for you! He is your defender.

6 He protects you day and night.

7 He keeps you from all evil, and preserves your life.

8 He keeps His eye upon you as you come and go, and always guards you.

GOD, YOU ARE HOLDING MY HAND
Psalm 73

23 But even so, You love me! You are holding my right hand!

24 You will keep on guiding me all my life with Your wisdom and counsel; and afterwards receive me into the glories of heaven!

25 Whom have I in heaven but You? And I desire no one on earth as much as You!

26 My health fails; my spirits droop, yet God remains! He is the strength of my heart; He is mine forever!

YOU WATCH OVER MY LIFE, GOD
Psalm 33

13,14,15 The Lord gazes down upon mankind from heaven where He lives. He has made their hearts and closely watches everything they do.

5

When You Feel
GUILTY AND SINFUL

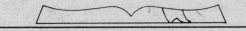

MIND RENEWAL PROMISE:
Romans 3

24 Yet now God declares us "not guilty" of offending Him if we trust in Jesus Christ, who in His kindness freely takes away our sins.

EVERYBODY SINS
Ecclesiastes 7

20 And there is not a single man in all the earth who is always good and never sins.

Romans 3

23 Yes, all have sinned; all fall short of God's glorious ideal.

GOD CAN FORGIVE
John 3

16 For God loved the world so much that He gave His only Son so that anyone who believes in Him shall not perish but have eternal life.

17 God did not send His Son into the world to condemn it, but to save it.

18 There is no eternal doom awaiting those who trust Him to save them.

GOD'S SURE FORGIVENESS
Hebrews 6

16 When a man takes an oath, he is calling upon someone greater than himself to force him to do what he has promised, or to punish him if he later refuses to do it; the oath ends all argument about it.

17 God also bound Himself with an oath, so that those He promised to help would be perfectly sure and never need to wonder whether He might change His plans.

18 He has given us both His promise and His oath, two things we can completely count on, for it is impossible for God to tell a lie. Now all those who flee to Him to save them can take new courage when they hear such assurances from God; now they can know without doubt that He will give them the salvation He has promised them.

19 This certain hope of being saved is a strong and trustworthy anchor for our souls, connecting us with God Himself behind the sacred curtains of heaven,

20 where Christ has gone ahead to plead for us from His position as our High Priest, with the honor and rank of Melchizedek.

EXAMPLES OF GOD'S FORGIVENESS
John 8

4 "Teacher," they said to Jesus, "this woman was caught in the very act of adultery.

5 Moses' law says to kill her. What about it?"

7 They kept demanding an answer, so He stood up again and said, "All right, hurl the stones at her

until she dies. But only he who never sinned may throw the first!"

9 And the Jewish leaders slipped away one by one, beginning with the eldest, until only Jesus was left in front of the crowd with the woman.

10 Then Jesus stood up again and said to her, "Where are your accusers? Didn't even one of them condemn you?"

11 "No, sir," she said.

And Jesus said, "Neither do I. Go and sin no more."

Luke 15

11 A man had two sons.

12 When the younger told his father, "I want my share of your estate now, instead of waiting until you die!" his father agreed to divide his wealth between his sons.

13 A few days later this younger son packed all his belongings and took a trip to a distant land, and there wasted all his money on parties and prostitutes.

14 About the time his money was gone a great famine swept over the land, and he began to starve.

15 He persuaded a local farmer to hire him to feed his pigs.

16 The boy became so hungry that even the pods he was feeding the swine looked good to him. And no one gave him anything.

17,18 When he finally came to his senses, he said to himself, "At home even the hired men have food enough and to spare, and here I am, dying of hunger! I will go home to my father and say, 'Father, I have sinned against both heaven and you,

19 I am no longer worthy of being called your son. Please take me on as a hired man.'"

20 So he returned home to his father. And while he was still a long distance away, his father saw him coming, and was filled with loving pity and ran and embraced him and kissed him.

21 His son said to him, "Father, I have sinned against heaven and you, and am not worthy of being called your son—"

22 But his father said to the slaves, "Quick! Bring the finest robe in the house and put it on him. And a jeweled ring for his finger; and shoes!

23 And kill the calf we have in the fattening pen. We must celebrate with a feast,

24 For this son of mine was dead and has returned to life..."

HOW TO PRAY FOR FORGIVENESS
Psalm 51

1 O loving and kind God, have mercy. Have pity upon me and take away the awful stain of my transgressions.

2 Oh, wash me, cleanse me from this guilt. Let me be pure again.

3 For I admit my shameful deed—it haunts me day and night.

4 It is against You and You alone I sinned, and did this terrible thing. You saw it all, and Your sentence against me is just.

7 Sprinkle me with the cleansing blood and I shall be clean again. Wash me and I shall be whiter than snow.

Psalm 130

1 O Lord, from the depths of despair I cry for Your help.

2 "Hear me! Answer! Help me!"

3,4 Lord, if You keep in mind our sins then who can ever get an answer to his prayers? But You forgive! What an awesome thing this is!

THE "HOW" OF BEING FORGIVEN

Not by works:
Romans 3

20 Now do you see it? No one can ever be made right in God's sight by doing what the law commands. For the more we know of God's laws, the clearer it becomes that we aren't obeying them; His laws serve only to make us see that we are sinners.

21,22 But now God has shown us a different way to heaven—not by "being good enough" and trying to keep His laws, but by a new way (though not new, really, for the Scriptures told about it long ago). Now God says He will accept and acquit us—declare us "not guilty"—if we trust Jesus Christ to take away our sins. And we all can be saved in this same way, by coming to Christ, no matter who we are or what we have been like.

27 Then what can we boast about doing, to earn our salvation? Nothing at all. Why? Because our acquittal is not based on our good deeds; it is based on what Christ has done and our faith in Him.

28 So it is that we are saved by faith in Christ and not by the good things we do.

Forgiven by confession:
1 John 1

8 If we say that we have no sin, we are only fooling ourselves, and refusing to accept the truth.

9 But if we confess our sins to Him, He can be depended on to forgive us and to cleanse us from every wrong. [And it is perfectly proper for God to do this for us because Christ died to wash away our sins.]

Psalm 32

1 What happiness for those whose guilt has been forgiven! What joys when sins are covered over! What relief for those who have confessed their sins and God has cleared their record.

3 There was a time when I wouldn't admit what a sinner I was. But my dishonesty made me miserable and filled my days with frustration.

4 All day and all night Your hand was heavy on me. My strength evaporated like water on a sunny day

5 Until I finally admitted all my sins to You and stopped trying to hide them. I said to myself, "I will confess them to the Lord." And You forgave me! All my guilt is gone.

6 Now I say that each believer should confess his sins to God when he is aware of them, while there is time to be forgiven. Judgment will not touch him if he does.

Now, grab the forgiveness by faith:

Acts 13

38 Brothers! Listen! In this man Jesus, there is forgiveness for your sins!

39 Everyone who trusts in Him is freed from all guilt and declared righteous.

AS FAR AS EAST FROM WEST
Psalm 103

1 I bless the holy name of God with all my heart.

2 Yes, I will bless the Lord and not forget the glorious things He does for me.

3 He forgives all my sins. He heals me.

8 He is merciful and tender toward those who don't deserve it; He is slow to get angry and full of kindness and love.

9 He never bears a grudge, nor remains angry forever.

10 He has not punished us as we deserve for all our sins,

11 For His mercy toward those who fear and honor Him is as great as the height of the heavens above the earth.

12 He has removed our sins as far away from us as the east is from the west.

YOU! ABSOLUTELY FLAWLESS THROUGH CHRIST!
Colossians 1

21 You were His enemies and hated Him and were separated from Him by your evil thoughts and actions, yet now He has brought you back as His friends.

22 He has done this through the death on the cross of His own human body, and now as a result Christ has brought you into the very presence of God, and you are standing there before Him with nothing left against you—nothing left that He could even chide you for:

23 The only condition is that you fully believe the Truth, standing in it steadfast and firm, strong in the Lord, convinced of the Good News that Jesus died for you, and never shifting from trusting Him to save you.

THE RECORD CLEARED—NO DAMNATION
John 5

24 "I say emphatically that anyone who listens to My message and believes in God who sent Me has eternal life, and will never be damned for his sins, but has already passed out of death into life."

GOD'S FORGIVENESS IS FOREVER
1 Corinthians 1

8 And He guarantees right up to the end that you will be counted free from all sin and guilt on that day when He returns.

9 God will surely do this for you, for He always does just what He says, and He is the one who invited you into this wonderful friendship with His Son, even Christ our Lord.

WHEN YOU CAN'T FORGIVE YOURSELF
Romans 8

30 And having chosen us, He called us to come to Him; and when we came, He declared us "not guilty," filled us with Christ's goodness, gave us right standing with Himself, and promised us His glory.

33 Who dares accuse us whom God has chosen for His own? Will God? No! He is the one who has forgiven us and given us right standing with Himself.

34 Who then will condemn us? Will Christ? *No!* For He is the one who died for us and came back to life again for us and is sitting at the place of highest honor next to God, pleading for us there in heaven.

LEFTOVER GUILT COMES FROM SATAN...REBUKE HIM!
Colossians 2

13 You were dead in sins, and your sinful desires were not yet cut away. Then He gave you a share in the very life of Christ, for He forgave all your sins,

14 And blotted out the charges proved against you, the list of His commandments which you had not obeyed. He took this list of sins and destroyed it by nailing it to Christ's cross.

15 In this way God took away Satan's power to accuse you of sin, and God openly displayed to the whole world Christ's triumph at the cross where your sins were all taken away.

MEMORIZE FOR EXTRA HELP
2 Corinthians 5

17 When someone becomes a Christian he becomes a brand new person inside. He is not the same any more. A new life has begun!

18 All these new things are from God who brought us back to Himself through what Christ Jesus did. And God has given us the privilege of urging everyone to come into His favor and be reconciled to Him.

19 For God was in Christ, restoring the world to Himself, no longer counting men's sins against them but blotting them out. This is the wonderful message He has given us to tell others.

21 For God took the sinless Christ and poured into Him our sins. Then, in exchange, He poured God's goodness into us!

6

When You Feel
HAPPY, THANKFUL

MIND RENEWAL PROMISE:
Psalm 118

29 Oh, give thanks to the Lord for He is so good! For His lovingkindness is forever.

LET'S PRAISE THE LORD!!
Psalm 104

33 I will sing to the Lord as long as I live. I will praise God to my last breath!

34 May He be pleased by all these thoughts about Him, for He is the source of all my joy.

35 Let all sinners perish—all who refuse to praise Him. But I will praise Him. Hallelujah!

GLORY TO YOUR NAME, O GOD!!
Psalm 108

1 O God, my heart is ready to praise You! I will sing and rejoice before You.

2 Wake up, O harp and lyre! We will meet the dawn with song.

3 I will praise You everywhere around the world, in every nation.

4 For Your lovingkindness is great beyond measure, high as the heavens. Your faithfulness reaches the skies.

5 His glory is far more vast than the heavens. It towers above the earth.

Psalm 145

1,2 I will praise You, my God and King, and bless Your name each day and forever.

3 Great is Jehovah! Greatly praise Him! His greatness is beyond discovery!

4 Let each generation tell its children what glorious things He does.

5 I will meditate about Your glory, splendor, majesty and miracles.

6 Your awe-inspiring deeds shall be on every tongue; I will proclaim Your greatness.

7 Everyone will tell about how good You are, and sing about Your righteousness.

8 Jehovah is kind and merciful, slow to get angry, full of love.

9 He is good to everyone, and His compassion is intertwined with everything He does.

10 All living things shall thank You, Lord, and Your people will bless You.

11 They will talk together about the glory of Your kingdom and mention examples of Your power.

12 They will tell about Your miracles and about the majesty and glory of Your reign.

13 For Your kingdom never ends. You rule generation after generation.

HALLELUJAH!!
Psalm 150

1 Hallelujah! Yes, praise the Lord!
Praise Him in His Temple, and in the heavens He made with mighty power.

2 Praise Him for His mighty works. Praise His unequaled greatness.

3 Praise Him with the trumpet and with lute and harp.

4 Praise Him with the tambourines and processional. Praise Him with stringed instruments and horns.

5 Praise Him with the cymbals, yes, loud clanging cymbals.

6 Let everything alive give praises to the Lord! *You* praise Him! Hallelujah!

LET EVERYTHING HE HAS MADE GIVE PRAISE TO HIM
Psalm 148

1 Praise the Lord, O heavens! Praise Him from the skies!

2 Praise Him, all His angels, all the armies of heaven.

3 Praise Him sun and moon, and all you twinkling stars.

4 Praise Him, skies above. Praise Him, vapors high above the clouds.

5 Let everything He has made give praise to Him! For He issued His command, and they came into being;

6 He established them forever and forever. His orders will never be revoked.

7 And praise Him down here on earth, you creatures of the ocean depths.

8 Let fire and hail, snow, rain, wind and weather, all obey.

9 Let the mountains and hills, the fruit trees and cedars,

10 The wild animals and cattle, the snakes and birds,

11 The kings and all the people, with their rulers and their judges,

12 Young men and maidens, old men and children—

13 All praise the Lord together. For He alone is worthy. His glory is far greater than all of earth and heaven.

BLESS THE LORD, O MY SOUL!!
Psalm 8

1 O Lord our God, the majesty and glory of Your name fills all the earth and overflows the heavens.

2 You have taught the little children to praise You perfectly. May their example shame and silence Your enemies!

3 When I look up into the night skies and see the work of Your fingers—the moon and the stars You have made—

4 I cannot understand how You can bother with mere puny man, to pay any attention to him!

5 And yet You have made him only a little lower than the angels, and placed a crown of glory and honor upon his head.

6 You have put him in charge of everything You made; everything is put under his authority:

7 All sheep and oxen, and wild animals too,

8 The birds and fish, and all the life in the sea.

9 O Jehovah, our Lord, the majesty and glory of Your name fills the earth.

HOW GREAT THOU ART!!
Psalm 104

1,2 I bless the Lord: O Lord my God, how great You are! You are robed with honor and with majesty and light! You stretched out the starry curtain of the heavens,

3 And hollowed out the surface of the earth to form the seas. The clouds are His chariots. He rides upon the wings of the wind.

4 The angels are His messengers—His servants of fire!

5 You bound the world together so that it would never fall apart.

6 You clothed the earth with floods of waters covering up the mountains.

7,8 You spoke, and at the sound of Your shout the water collected into its vast ocean beds, and mountains rose and valleys sank to the levels You decreed.

9 And then You set a boundary for the seas, so that they would never again cover the earth.

10 He placed springs in the valleys, and streams that gush from the mountains.

11 They give water for all the animals to drink. There the wild donkeys quench their thirst.

12 And the birds nest beside the streams and sing among the branches of the trees.

13 He sends rain upon the mountains and fills the earth with fruit.

14 The tender grass grows up at His command to feed the cattle, and there are fruit trees, vegetables and grain for man to cultivate.

15 And wine to make him glad, and olive oil as lotion for his skin, and bread to give him strength.

16 The Lord planted the cedars of Lebanon. They are tall and flourishing.

17 There the birds make their nests, the storks in the firs.

18 High in the mountains are pastures for the wild goats, and rock-badgers burrow in among the rocks and find protection there.

19 He assigned the moon to mark the months, and the sun to mark the days.

20 He sends the night and darkness, when all the forest folk come out.

21 Then the young lions roar for their food, but they are dependent on the Lord.

22 At dawn they slink back into their dens to rest.

23 And men go off to work until the evening shadows fall again.

PRAISE GOD FOREVER!!
Psalm 105

1 Thank the Lord for all the glorious things He does; proclaim them to the nations.

2 Sing His praises and tell everyone about His miracles.

3 Glory in the Lord; O worshipers of God, rejoice.

7 He is the Lord our God. His goodness is seen everywhere throughout the land.

THE EARTH IS FULL OF YOUR RICHES, O LORD!
Psalm 104

24 O Lord, what a variety You have made! And in wisdom You have made them all! The earth is full of Your riches.

25 There before me lies the mighty ocean, teeming with life of every kind, both great and small.

26 And look! See the ships! And over there, the whale You made to play in the sea.

27 Every one of these depends on You to give them daily food.

28 You supply it, and they gather it. You open wide Your hand to feed them and they are satisfied with all Your bountiful provision.

29 But if You turn away from them, then all is lost. And when You gather up their breath, they die and turn again to dust.

30 Then You send Your Spirit, and new life is born to replenish all the living of the earth.

31 Praise God forever! How He must rejoice in all His work!

7

When You Feel
HURT, HUMILIATED

MIND RENEWAL PROMISE:
Psalm 147

3 He heals the brokenhearted, binding up their wounds.

GOD KNOWS YOUR HURT
Psalm 34

18 The Lord is close to those whose hearts are breaking; He rescues those who are humbly sorry for their sins.

19 The good man does not escape all troubles—he has them too. But the Lord helps him in each and every one.

GOD YEARNS TO HELP
2 Chronicles 16

9 For the eyes of the Lord search back and forth across the whole earth, looking for people whose hearts are perfect toward Him, so that He can show His great power in helping them.

CHRIST WAS HURT TOO
1 Peter 2

19 Praise the Lord if you are punished for doing right!

20 Of course, you get no credit for being patient if you are beaten for doing wrong; but if you do right and suffer for it, and are patient beneath the blows, God is well pleased.

21 This suffering is all part of the work God has given you. Christ, who suffered for you, is your example. Follow in His steps:

22 He never sinned, never told a lie,

23 Never answered back when insulted; when He suffered He did not threaten to get even; He left His case in the hands of God who always judges fairly.

24 He personally carried the load of our sins in His own body when He died on the cross, so that we can be finished with sin and live a good life from now on. For His wounds have healed ours!

GOD'S LOVE REMAINS CONSTANT
Psalm 33

18, 19 But the eyes of the Lord are watching over those who fear Him, who rely upon His steady love. He will keep them from death even in times of famine!

22 Yes, Lord, let Your constant love surround us, for our hopes are in You alone.

Deuteronomy 31

8 ...The Lord will go before you and will be with you; He will not fail nor forsake you.

GOD UNDERSTANDS
Ephesians 1

8 And He has showered down upon us the richness of His grace—for how well He understands us and knows what is best for us at all times.

QUIETLY TRUST YOUR CASE TO GOD
1 Peter 3

15 Quietly trust yourself to Christ your Lord and if anybody asks why you believe as you do, be ready to tell him, and do it in a gentle and respectful way.

16 Do what is right; then if men speak against you, calling you evil names, they will become ashamed of themselves for falsely accusing you when you have only done what is good.

17 Remember, if God wants you to suffer, it is better to suffer for doing good than for doing wrong!

18 Christ also suffered.

GOD IS A STRONG, SAFE PLACE WHEN YOU ARE HURTING
Psalm 18

2 The Lord is my fort where I can enter and be safe; no one can follow me in and slay me. He is a rugged mountain where I hide; He is my Savior, a rock where none can reach me, and a tower of safety. He is my shield. He is like the strong horn of a mighty fighting bull.

"I HAVE OVERCOME THE WORLD"...Jesus
John 16

33b ...."Here on earth you will have many trials and sorrows; but cheer up, for I have overcome the world."

COMFORTER
John 14

16 I will ask the Father and He will give you another Comforter, and He will never leave you.

17 He is the Holy Spirit...

18 No, I will not abandon you or leave you as orphans in the storm—I will come to you.

THOSE WHO MOURN ARE FORTUNATE
Matthew 5

1,2 One day as the crowds were gathering, He went up the hillside with His disciples and sat down and taught them there.

3 "Humble men are very fortunate!" He told them, "for the Kingdom of Heaven is given to them.

4 Those who mourn are fortunate! for they shall be comforted.

5 The meek and lowly are fortunate! for the whole wide world belongs to them."

COMFORTING WORDS
Joshua 23

10 The Lord your God fights for you, just as He has promised.

POWERFUL THOUGHTS
Psalm 42

1 As the deer pants for water, so I long for You, O God.

2 I thirst for God, the living God. Where can I find Him to come and stand before Him?

3 Day and night I weep for His help, and all the while my enemies taunt me. "Where is this God of yours?" they scoff.

7 All your waves and billows have gone over me, and floods of sorrow pour upon me like a thundering cataract.

8 Yet day by day the Lord also pours out His steadfast love upon me, and through the night I

sing His songs and pray to God who gives me life.

HEAR YE!!
Romans 11

33 Oh, what a wonderful God we have! How great are His wisdom and knowledge and riches! How impossible it is for us to understand His decisions and His methods!

34 For who among us can know the mind of the Lord? Who knows enough to be His counselor and guide?

35 And who could ever offer to the Lord enough to induce Him to act?

36 For everything comes from God alone. Everything lives by His power, and everything is for His glory. To Him be glory evermore.

8

When You Feel IMPATIENT

MIND RENEWAL PROMISE:
James 1

3 ...when the way is rough, your patience has a chance to grow.

4 So let it grow, and don't try to squirm out of your problems. For when your patience is finally in full bloom, then you will be ready for anything, strong in character, full and complete.

WHY WORRY?
GOD IS NOT HURRIED OR HARRIED

Psalm 90

1 Lord, through all the generations You have been our home!

2 Before the mountains were created, before the earth was formed, You are God without beginning or end.

3 You speak, and man turns back to dust.

4 A thousand years are but as yesterday to You! They are like a single hour!

5,6 We glide along the tides of time as swiftly as a racing river, and vanish as quickly as a dream. We are like grass that is green in the morning but mowed down and withered before the evening shadows fall.

Psalm 37

34 Don't be impatient for the Lord to act! Keep traveling steadily along His pathway and in due season He will honor you with every blessing, and you will see the wicked destroyed.

35 I myself have seen it happen.

THERE IS A RIGHT TIME FOR EVERYTHING
Ecclesiastes 3

1 There is a right time for everything:
2 A time to be born, a time to die;
  A time to plant;
  A time to harvest;
3 A time to kill;
  A time to heal;
  A time to destroy,
  A time to rebuild;
4 A time to cry;
  A time to laugh;
  A time to grieve;
  A time to dance;
5 A time for scattering stones;
  A time for gathering stones;
  A time to hug;
  A time not to hug;
6 A time to find;
  A time to lose;
  A time for keeping;
  A time for throwing away;
7 A time to tear;
  A time to repair;
  A time to be quiet;
  A time to speak up;

8 A time for loving;
A time for hating;
A time for war;
A time for peace.

HOW TO KEEP FROM GETTING WEARY WHILE WAITING
Hebrews 12

1 Since we have such a huge crowd of men of faith watching us from the grandstands, let us strip off anything that slows us down or holds us back, and especially those sins that wrap themselves so tightly around our feet and trip us up; and let us run with patience the particular race that God has set before us.

2 Keep your eyes on Jesus, our leader and instructor. He was willing to die a shameful death on the cross because of the joy He knew would be His afterwards; and now He sits in the place of honor by the throne of God.

3 If you want to keep from becoming faint-hearted and weary, think about His patience as sinful men did such terrible things to Him.

4 After all, you have never yet struggled against sin and temptation until you sweat great drops of blood.

PRAISE HIM THROUGH IT ALL!
Romans 12

12 Be glad for all God is planning for you. Be patient in trouble, and prayerful always.

PATIENCE FROM CHRIST
2 Thessalonians 3

5 May the Lord bring you into an ever deeper understanding of the love of God and of the patience that comes from Christ.

PATIENCE FROM THE HOLY SPIRIT
Galatians 5

22 But when the Holy Spirit controls our lives He will produce this kind of fruit in us: love, joy, peace, patience, kindness, goodness, faithfulness,

23 gentleness and self-control; and here there is no conflict with Jewish laws.

25 If we are living now by the Holy Spirit's power, let us follow the Holy Spirit's leading in every part of our lives.

PATIENCE FROM UNSELFISHNESS
2 Peter 1

6 Next, learn to put aside your own desires so that you will become patient and godly, gladly letting God have His way with you.

PATIENCE FROM TROUBLE
Romans 5

3 We can rejoice, too, when we run into problems and trials for we know that they are good for us—they help us learn to be patient.

4 And patience develops strength of character in us and helps us trust God more each time we use it until finally our hope and faith are strong and steady.

5 Then, when that happens, we are able to hold our heads high no matter what happens and know that all is well, for we know how dearly God loves us, and we feel this warm love everywhere within us because God has given us the Holy Spirit to fill our hearts with His love.

PATIENCE FROM EXPECTATION
Psalm 42

11 But O my soul, don't be discouraged. Don't be upset. Expect God to act! For I know that I shall again have plenty of reason to praise Him for all that He will do. He is my help! He is my God!

PATIENCE AND PEACE FROM "KEEPING ON TRUSTING"
Romans 8

25 But if we must keep trusting God for something that hasn't happened yet, it teaches us to wait patiently and confidently.

Isaiah 26

2 Open the gates to everyone, for all may enter in who love the Lord.

3 He will keep in perfect peace all those who trust in Him, whose thoughts turn often to the Lord!

4 Trust in the Lord God always, for in the Lord Jehovah is your everlasting strength.

PAUL'S PATIENCE
Philippians 4

12 I know how to live on almost nothing or with everything. I have learned the secret of contentment in every situation, whether it be a full stomach or hunger, plenty or want.

JOB'S ATTITUDE WHILE WAITING
Job 1

21b ...The Lord gave me everything I had, and they were His to take away. Blessed be the name of the Lord.

Job 13

15 Though He slay me, yet will I trust Him.

JOY WHEN THE WAITING IS OVER
Psalm 40

1 I waited patiently for God to help me; then He listened and heard my cry.

2 He lifted me out of the pit of despair, out from the bog and the mire, and set my feet on a hard, firm path and steadied me as I walked along.

3 He has given me a new song to sing, of praises to our God. Now many will hear of the glorious things He did for me, and stand in awe before the Lord, and put their trust in Him.

4 Many blessings are given to those who trust the Lord, and have no confidence in those who are proud, or who trust in idols.

5 O Lord my God, many and many a time You have done great miracles for us, and we are ever in Your thoughts. Who else can do such glorious things? No one else can be compared with You. There isn't time to tell of all Your wonderful deeds.

Jonah 2

5 I sank beneath the waves, and death was very near. The waters closed above me; the seaweed wrapped itself around my head.

6 I went down to the bottoms of the mountains that rise from off the ocean floor. I was locked out of life and imprisoned in the land of death. But, O Lord my God, You have snatched me from the yawning jaws of death!

7 When I had lost all hope, I turned my thoughts once more to the Lord. And my earnest prayer went to You in Your holy Temple.

9 I will never worship anyone but You! For how can I thank You enough for all You have done! I will surely fulfill my promises.

MORE JOY
Psalm 98

1 Sing a new song to the Lord telling about His mighty deeds! For He has won a mighty victory by His power and holiness.

5 Sing your praise accompanied by music from the harp.

6 Let the cornets and trumpets shout! Make a joyful symphony before the Lord, the King!

7 Let the sea in all its vastness roar with praise! Let the earth and all those living on it shout, "Glory to the Lord."

8,9 Let the waves clap their hands in glee, and the hills sing out their songs of joy before the Lord.

9

When You Feel
LIFE IS MEANINGLESS, WITHOUT PURPOSE

MIND RENEWAL PROMISE:
Ephesians 2

10 It is God Himself who has made us what we are and given us new lives from Christ Jesus; and long ages ago He planned that we should spend these lives in helping others.

WHY GOD MADE YOU

To glorify God:
Isaiah 43

7 All who claim Me as their God will come, for I have made them for My glory; I created them.

To seek after God:
Acts 17

26 He created all the people of the world from one man, Adam, and scattered the nations across the face of the earth. He decided beforehand which should rise and fall, and when. He determined their boundaries.

27 His purpose in all of this is that they should seek after God, and perhaps feel their way toward Him and find Him—though He is not far from any one of us.

To know God:
1 Timothy 6

20 Keep out of foolish arguments with those who boast of their "knowledge" and thus prove their lack of it.

21 Some of these people have missed the most important thing in life—they don't know God. May God's mercy be upon you.

To praise God:
Ephesians 1

11 Moreover, because of what Christ has done we have become gifts to God that He delights in, for as part of God's sovereign plan we were chosen from the beginning to be His, and all things happen just as He decided long ago.

12 God's purpose in this was that we should praise God and give glory to Him for doing these mighty things for us, who were the first to trust in Christ.

Psalm 22

28 For the Lord is King and rules the nations.

29 Both proud and humble together, all who are mortal—born to die—shall worship Him.

To love God:
Mark 12

28 One of the teachers of religion who was standing there listening to the discussion realized that Jesus had answered well. So he asked, "Of all the commandments, which is the most important?"

29 Jesus replied, "The one that says, 'Hear, O Israel! The Lord our God is the one and only God.

30 And you must love Him with all your heart and soul and mind and strength.'

31 The second is: 'You must love others as much as yourself.' No other commandments are greater than these."

To love others:
1 Peter 1

22 Now you can have real love for everyone because your souls have been cleansed from selfishness and hatred when you trusted Christ to save you; so see to it that you really do love each other warmly, with all your hearts.

Philippians 2

3 Don't be selfish; don't live to make a good impression on others. Be humble, thinking of others as better than yourself.

4 Don't just think about your own affairs, but be interested in others, too, and in what they are doing.

5 Your attitude should be the kind that was shown us by Jesus Christ,

6 Who, though He was God, did not demand and cling to His rights as God,

7 But laid aside His mighty power and glory, taking the disguise of a slave and becoming like men.

8 And He humbled Himself even further, going so far as actually to die a criminal's death on a cross.

9 Yet it was because of this that God raised Him up to the heights of heaven and gave Him a name which is above every other name.

To please God:
2 Corinthians 5

9 So our aim is to please Him always in everything we do, whether we are here in this body or away from this body and with Him in heaven.

15 He died for all so that all who live—having received eternal life from Him—might live no longer for themselves, to please themselves, but to spend their lives pleasing Christ who died and rose again for them.

Psalm 40

6 It isn't sacrifices and offerings which You really want from Your people. Burnt animals bring no special joy to Your heart. But You have accepted the offer of my lifelong service.

To obey God:
1 Peter 1

14 Obey God because you are His children; don't slip back into your old ways—doing evil because you knew no better.

15 But be holy now in everything you do, just as the Lord is holy, who invited you to be His child.

16 He Himself has said, "You must be holy, for I am holy."

To do good:
Amos 5

21 I hate your show and pretense—your hypocrisy of "honoring" Me with your religious feasts and solemn assemblies.

24 I want to see a mighty flood of justice—a torrent of doing good.

To trust God:
Psalm 50

14,15 What I want from you is your true thanks; I want your promises fulfilled. *I want you to trust Me in your times of trouble, so I can rescue you, and you can give Me glory.*

To tell the Gospel:
2 Corinthians 4

1 It is God Himself, in His mercy, who has given us this wonderful work [of telling His Good News to others], and so we never give up.

5 We don't go around preaching about ourselves, but about Christ Jesus as Lord. All we say of ourselves is that we are your slaves because of what Jesus has done for us.

John 4

34 Then Jesus explained: "My nourishment comes from doing the will of God who sent Me, and from finishing His work.

35 Do you think the work of harvesting will not begin until the summer ends four months from now? Look around you! Vast fields of human souls are ripening all around us, and are ready now for reaping.

36 The reapers will be paid good wages and will be gathering eternal souls into the granaries of heaven! What joys await the sower and the reaper, both together!"

REAL SATISFACTION
Mark 8

34 Then He called His disciples and the crowds to come over and listen. "If any of you wants to be

My follower," He told them, "you must put aside your own pleasures and shoulder your cross, and follow Me closely.

35 If you insist on saving your life, you will lose it. Only those who throw away their lives for My sake and for the sake of the Good News will ever know what it means to really live."

GOOD MEN ENJOY LIFE
Proverbs 2

20 Follow the steps of the godly instead, and stay on the right path.

21 For only good men enjoy life to the full;

22 Evil men lose the good things they might have had, and they themselves shall be destroyed.

ABUNDANT LIFE
1 Corinthians 4

20 The kingdom of God is not just talking; it is living by God's power.

REAL FULFILLMENT
Matthew 20

26 But among you it is quite different. Anyone wanting to be a leader among you must be your servant.

27 And if you want to be right at the top, you must serve like a slave.

28 Your attitude must be like My own, for I, the Son of Mankind, did not come to be served, but to serve, and to give My life as a ransom for many.

HIS WAYS SATISFY
Romans 12

1 And so, dear brothers, I plead with you to give your bodies to God. Let them be a living sacrifice, holy—the kind He can accept. When you think of what He has done for you, is this too much to ask?

2 Don't copy the behavior and customs of this world, but be a new and different person with a fresh newness in all you do and think. Then you will learn from your own experience how His ways will really satisfy you.

10

When You Feel
RESENTFUL, HATEFUL, GRUDGING

MIND RENEWAL PROMISE:
Matthew 6

14,15 Your heavenly Father will forgive you if you forgive those who sin against you; but if *you* refuse to forgive *them, He* will not forgive *you.*

YOU CANNOT HIDE
HOSTILITY AND RESENTMENT
Proverbs 26

24,25,26 A man with hate in his heart may sound pleasant enough, but don't believe him; for he is cursing you in his heart. Though he pretends to be so kind, his hatred will finally come to light for all to see.

HATE DESTROYS FRIENDSHIPS
Proverbs 18

19 It is harder to win back the friendship of an offended brother than to capture a fortified city.

BITTERNESS DESTROYS SPIRITUALITY
Hebrews 12

15b ...Watch out that no bitterness takes root among you, for as it springs up it causes deep trouble, hurting many in their spiritual lives.

DON'T LET THE SUN GO DOWN
ON YOUR ANGER
Ephesians 4

22 Then throw off your old evil nature—the old you that was a partner in your evil ways—rotten through and through, full of lust and sham.

23 Now your attitudes and thoughts must all be constantly changing for the better.

24 Yes, you must be a new and different person, holy and good. Clothe yourself with this new nature.

26 If you are angry, don't sin by nursing your grudge. Don't let the sun go down with you still angry—get over it quickly;

27 For when you are angry you give a mighty foothold to the devil.

31 Stop being mean, bad-tempered and angry. Quarreling, harsh words, and dislike of others should have no place in your lives.

32 Instead, be kind to each other, tenderhearted, forgiving one another, just as God has forgiven you because you belong to Christ.

SEVENTY TIMES SEVEN!!
Matthew 18

21 Then Peter came to Him and asked, "Sir, how often should I forgive a brother who sins against me? Seven times?"

22 "No!" Jesus replied, "seventy times seven!"

SOME DISTINCTIVE THERAPY
Luke 6

27 Listen, all of you. Love your *enemies*. Do *good* to those who *hate* you.

28 Pray for the happiness of those who *curse* you; implore God's blessing on those who *hurt* you.

29 If someone slaps you on one cheek, let him slap the other too! If someone demands your coat, give him your shirt besides.

30 Give what you have to anyone who asks you for it; and when things are taken away from you, don't worry about getting them back.

31 Treat others as you want them to treat you.

33 And if you do good only to those who do you good—is that so wonderful? Even sinners do that much!

34 And if you lend money only to those who can repay you, what good is that? Even the most wicked will lend to their own kind for full return!

35 Love your *enemies!* Do good to *them!* Lend to *them!* And don't be concerned about the fact that they won't repay. Then your reward from heaven will be very great, and you will truly be acting as sons of God: for He is kind to the *unthankful* and to those who are *very wicked*.

36 Try to show as much compassion as your Father does.

WHEN YOU ARE INSULTED OR PUT DOWN..(CHRIST AS EXAMPLE)
1 Peter 2

22 He never sinned, never told a lie,

23 Never answered back when insulted; when He suffered He did not threaten to get even; He left His case in the hands of God who always judges fairly.

WHY SHOULD I GIVE UP RESENTMENT?

Because God said to do it:
Colossians 3

13 Be gentle and ready to forgive; never hold grudges. Remember, the Lord forgave you, so you must forgive others.

Because God is watching:
1 Peter 3

11 Turn away from evil and do good. Try to live in peace even if you must run after it to catch and hold it!

12 For the Lord is watching His children, listening to their prayers; but the Lord's face is hard against those who do evil.

Because your behavior will be judged:
2 Corinthians 5

10 For we must all stand before Christ to be judged and have our lives laid bare—before Him. Each of us will receive whatever he deserves for the good or bad things he has done in his earthly body.

Hebrews 10

31 It is a fearful thing to fall into the hands of the living God.

Because God will reward you:
Proverbs 25

21,22 If your enemy is hungry, give him food! If he is thirsty, give him something to drink! This will make him feel ashamed of himself, and God will reward you.

To keep Satan's hand away:
2 Corinthians 2

11 A further reason for forgiveness is to keep from being outsmarted by Satan.

God will handle justice:
Hebrews 10

30 For we know Him who said, "Justice belongs to Me; I will repay them"; who also said, "The Lord Himself will handle these cases."

Romans 12

19 Dear friends, never avenge yourselves. Leave that to God, for He has said that He will repay those who deserve it.

POWERFUL THOUGHTS
Matthew 5

46 If you love only those who love you, what good is that? Even scoundrels do that much.

47 If you are friendly only to your friends, how are you different from anyone else? Even the heathen do that.

1 John 4

20 If anyone says "I love God," but keeps on hating his brother, he is a liar; for if he doesn't love his brother who is right there in front of him, how can he love God whom he has never seen?

21 And God Himself has said that one must love not only God, but his brother too.

IMPORTANT!
Colossians 3

12 Since you have been chosen by God who has

given you this new kind of life, and because of His deep love and concern for you, you should practice tenderhearted mercy and kindness to others.

Ephesians 5

1 Follow God's example in everything you do just as a much loved child imitates his father.

2 Be full of love for others, following the example of Christ who loved you and gave Himself to God as a sacrifice to take away your sins. And God was pleased, for Christ's love for you was like sweet perfume to Him.

11

When You Feel
RESTLESS, UNEASY, WITHOUT PEACE

MIND RENEWAL PROMISE:
Jeremiah 6

16 Yet the Lord pleads with you still: Ask where the good road is, the godly paths you used to walk in, in the days of long ago. Travel there, and you will find rest for your souls.

GOD: ON RESTLESSNESS
Isaiah 57

15 The high and lofty one who inhabits eternity, the Holy One, says this: I live in that high and holy place where those with contrite, humble spirits dwell; and I refresh the humble and give new courage to those with repentant hearts.

18 I have seen what they do, but I will heal them anyway! I will lead them and comfort them, helping them to mourn and to confess their sins.

19 Peace, peace to them, both near and far, for I will heal them all.

20 But those who still reject Me are like the restless sea, which is never still, but always churns up mire and dirt.

21 There is no peace, says my God, for them!

NO PEACE WHILE HANGING ON TO SIN
Psalm 85

8 I am listening carefully to all the Lord is saying—for He speaks peace to His people, His saints, if they will only stop their sinning.

Proverbs 10

10 Winking at sin leads to sorrow; bold reproof leads to peace.

Proverbs 28

1 The wicked flee when no one is chasing them! But the godly are bold as lions!

ARE YOU RESTLESS BECAUSE YOU ARE BORED?
Proverbs 14

14 The backslider gets bored with himself; the godly man's life is exciting.

Hebrews 6

11 And we are anxious that you keep right on loving others as long as life lasts, so that you will get your full reward.

12 Then, knowing what lies ahead for you, you won't become bored with being a Christian, nor become spiritually dull and indifferent, but you will be anxious to follow the example of those who receive all that God has promised them because of their strong faith and patience.

Are you restless and uneasy because you feel afraid? Discouraged? Resentful? Guilty? Weak? Worthless? **Refer to appropriate chapter by using the Table of Contents.**

INNER PEACE—HOW?
Romans 8

5 Those who let themselves be controlled by their lower natures live only to please themselves, but those who follow after the Holy Spirit find themselves doing those things that please God.

6 Following after the Holy Spirit leads to life and peace, but following after the old nature leads to death.

RELIEF FROM A
RESTLESS, UNEASY SPIRIT
Romans 8

28 And we know that all that happens to us is working for our good if we love God and are fitting into His plans.

Psalm 37

1 Never envy the wicked!

2 Soon they fade away like grass and disappear.

3. Trust in the Lord instead. Be kind and good to others; then you will live safely here in the land and prosper, feeding in safety.

4 Be delighted in the Lord. Then He will give you all your heart's desires.

7 Rest in the Lord; wait patiently for Him to act. Don't be envious of evil men who prosper.

8 Stop your anger! Turn off your wrath. Don't fret and worry—it only leads to harm.

11 But all who humble themselves before the Lord shall be given every blessing, and shall have wonderful peace.

PEACE FROM GOD
Isaiah 26

3 He will keep in perfect peace all those who trust in Him, whose thoughts turn often to the Lord!

4 Trust in the Lord God always, for in the Lord Jehovah is your everlasting strength.

PEACE WITH GOD—HOW?
Colossians 1

20 It was through what His Son did that God cleared a path for everything to come to Him—all things in heaven and on earth—for Christ's death on the cross has made peace with God for all by His blood.

INSTRUCTIONS FOR LIVING PEACEFULLY WITH OTHERS
Romans 12

12 Be glad for all God is planning for you. Be patient in trouble and prayerful always.

13 When God's children are in need, you be the one to help them out. And get into the habit of inviting guests home for dinner or if they need lodging, for the night.

14 If someone mistreats you because you are a Christian, don't curse him; pray that God will bless him.

15 When others are happy, be happy with them. If they are sad, share their sorrow.

16 Work happily together. Don't try to act big. Don't try to get into the good graces of important people, but enjoy the company of ordinary folks. And don't think you know it all!

17 Never pay back evil for evil. Do things in such a way that everyone can see you are honest clear through.

18 Don't quarrel with anyone. Be at peace with everyone, just as much as possible.

19 Dear friends, never avenge yourselves. Leave that to God, for He has said that He will repay those who deserve it. (Don't take the law into your own hands.)

20 Instead, feed your enemy if he is hungry. If he is thirsty give him something to drink and you will be "heaping coals of fire on his head." In other words, he will feel ashamed of himself for what he has done to you.

21 Don't let evil get the upper hand but conquer evil by doing good.

HELPS AND HINTS FOR
LIVING IN PEACE WITH OTHERS
Proverbs 16

7 When a man is trying to please God, God makes even his worst enemies to be at peace with him.

Proverbs 17

9 Love forgets mistakes; nagging about them parts the best of friends.

James 3

17 But the wisdom that comes from heaven is first of all pure and full of quiet gentleness. Then it is peace-loving and courteous. It allows discussion and is willing to yield to others; it is full of mercy and good deeds. It is wholehearted and straight-forward and sincere.

18 And those who are peacemakers will plant seeds of peace and reap a harvest of goodness.

HOPE FOR PEACE IN THE FUTURE
Micah 4

1 But in the last days Mount Zion will be the most renowned of all the mountains of the world, praised by all nations; people from all over the world will make pilgrimages there.

2 "Come," they will say to one another, "let us visit the mountain of the Lord, and see the Temple of the God of Israel; He will tell us what to do, and we will do it." For in those days the whole world will be ruled by the Lord from Jerusalem! He will issue His laws and announce His decrees from there.

3 He will arbitrate among the nations, and dictate to strong nations far away. They will beat their swords into plowshares and their spears into pruning-hooks; nations shall no longer fight each other, for all war will end. There will be universal peace, and all the military academies and training camps will be closed down.

4 Everyone will live quietly in his own home in peace and prosperity, for there will be nothing to fear. The Lord Himself has promised this.

GOD'S REST
Hebrews 4

1 Although God's promise still stands—His promise that all may enter His place of rest—we ought to tremble with fear because some of you may be on the verge of failing to get there after all.

2 For this wonderful news—the message that God wants to save us—has been given to us just as

it was to those who lived in the time of Moses. But it didn't do them any good because they didn't believe it. They didn't mix it with faith.

3 For only we who believe God can enter into His place of rest. He has said, "I have sworn in My anger that those who don't believe Me will never get in," even though He has been ready and waiting for them since the world began.

9 So there is a full complete rest *still waiting* for the people of God.

10 Christ has already entered there. He is resting from His work, just as God did after the creation.

11 Let us do our best to go into that place of rest, too, being careful not to disobey God as the children of Israel did, thus failing to get in.

SCRIPTURES THAT PRODUCE PEACE
Psalm 34

7 For the Angel of the Lord guards and rescues all who reverence Him.

8 Oh, put God to the test and see how kind He is! See for yourself the way His mercies shower down on all who trust in Him.

9 If you belong to the Lord, reverence Him; for everyone who does this has everything he needs.

10 Even strong young lions sometimes go hungry, but those of us who reverence the Lord will never lack any good thing.

11 Sons and daughters, come and listen and let me teach you the importance of trusting and fearing the Lord.

Psalm 100

1 Shout with joy before the Lord, O earth!

2 Obey Him gladly; come before Him, singing with joy.

3 Try to realize what this means—the Lord is God! He made us—we are His people, the sheep of His pasture.

4 Go through His open gates with great thanksgiving; enter His courts with praise. Give thanks to Him and bless His name.

5 For the Lord is always good. He is always loving and kind, and His faithfulness goes on and on to each succeeding generation.

Psalm 62

1 I stand silently before the Lord, waiting for Him to rescue me. For salvation comes from Him alone.

2 Yes, He alone is my Rock, my rescuer, defense and fortress. Why then should I be tense with fear when troubles come?

Psalm 23

1 Because the Lord is my Shepherd, I have everything I need!

2,3 He lets me rest in the meadow grass and leads me beside the quiet streams. He restores my failing health. He helps me do what honors Him the most.

4 Even when walking through the dark valley of death I will not be afraid, for You are close beside me, guarding, guiding all the way.

5 You provide delicious food for me in the presence of my enemies. You have welcomed me as Your guest; blessings overflow!

6 Your goodness and unfailing kindness shall be with me all of my life, and afterwards I will live with You forever in Your home.

PEACE BENEDICTION
Numbers 6

24,25,26 May the Lord bless and protect you; may the Lord's face radiate with joy because of you; may He be gracious to you, show you His favor, and give you His peace.

Isaiah 26

12 Lord, grant us peace; for all we have and are has come from You.

When You Feel
SAD

MIND RENEWAL PROMISE:
Psalm 146

8 He opens the eyes of the blind; He lifts the burdens from those bent down beneath their loads. For the Lord loves good men.

GOD KNOWS AND CARES ABOUT YOUR SADNESS
Psalm 139

1 O Lord, You have examined my heart and know everything about me.

2 You know when I sit or stand. When far away you know my every thought.

3 You chart the path ahead of me, and tell me where to stop and rest. Every moment, You know where I am.

4 You know what I am going to say before I even say it.

17,18 How precious it is, Lord, to realize that You are thinking about me constantly! I can't even count how many times a day Your thoughts turn towards me. And when I waken in the morning, You are still thinking of me!

COMFORT: JESUS TOO EXPERIENCED GRIEF

Isaiah 53

2 In God's eyes He was like a tender green shoot, sprouting from a root in dry and sterile ground. But in our eyes there was no attractiveness at all, nothing to make us want Him.

3 We despised Him and rejected Him—a man of sorrows, acquainted with bitterest grief. We turned our backs on Him and looked the other way when He went by. He was despised and we didn't care.

4 Yet it was *our* grief He bore, *our* sorrows that weighed Him down. And we thought His troubles were a punishment from God, for His *own* sins!

5 But He was wounded and bruised for *our* sins. He was chastised that we might have peace; He was lashed—and we were healed!

7 He was oppressed and He was afflicted, yet He never said a word. He was brought as a lamb to the slaughter; and as a sheep before her shearers is dumb, so He stood silent before the ones condemning Him.

Hebrews 2

18 For since He Himself has now been through suffering and temptation, He knows what it is like when we suffer and are tempted, and He is wonderfully able to help us.

JESUS TOO EXPERIENCED SADNESS
Luke 13

34 "O Jerusalem, Jerusalem! The city that murders the prophets. The city that stones those sent to help her. How often I have wanted to

gather your children together even as a hen protects her brood under her wings, but you wouldn't let Me.

35 And now—now your house is left desolate. And you will never again see Me until you say, 'Welcome to Him who comes in the name of the Lord.'"

GOD USES SORROW
2 Corinthians 7

8 I am no longer sorry that I sent that letter to you, though I was very sorry for a time, realizing how painful it would be to you. But it hurt you only for a little while.

9 Now I am glad I sent it, not because it hurt you, but because the pain turned you to God. It was a good kind of sorrow you felt, the kind of sorrow God wants His people to have, so that I need not come to you with harshness.

10 For God sometimes uses sorrow in our lives to help us turn away from sin and seek eternal life. We should never regret His sending it.

Romans 5

3 We can rejoice, too, when we run into problems and trials for we know that they are good for us—they help us learn to be patient.

HEALER OF THE BROKENHEARTED
Luke 4

14 Then Jesus returned to Galilee, full of the Holy Spirit's power. Soon He became well known throughout all that region

15 For His sermons in the synagogues; everyone praised Him.

16 When He came to the village of Nazareth, His boyhood home, He went as usual to the synagogue on Saturday, and stood up to read the Scriptures.

17 The book of Isaiah the prophet was handed to Him and He opened it to the place where it says:

18,19 The Spirit of the Lord is upon me; He has appointed me to preach Good News to the poor; He has sent me to heal the brokenhearted and to announce that captives shall be released and the blind shall see, that the downtrodden shall be freed from their oppressors, and that God is ready to give blessings to all who come to Him.

20 He closed the book and handed it back to the attendant and sat down, while everyone in the synagogue gazed at Him intently.

21 Then He added, "These Scriptures came true today!"

RENEW YOUR STRENGTH
Isaiah 40

25 "With whom will you compare Me? Who is My equal?" asks the Holy One.

26 Look up into the heavens! Who created all these stars? As a shepherd leads his sheep, calling each by its pet name, and counts them to see that none are lost or strayed, so God does with stars and planets!

27 O Jacob, O Israel, how can you say that the Lord doesn't see your troubles and isn't being fair?

28 Don't you yet understand? Don't you know by now that the everlasting God, the Creator of the farthest parts of the earth, never grows faint or weary? No one can fathom the depths of His understanding.

29 He gives power to the tired and worn out, and strength to the weak.

30 Even the youths shall be exhausted, and the young men will all give up.

31 But they that wait upon the Lord shall renew their strength. They shall mount up with wings like eagles; they shall run and not be weary; they shall walk and not faint.

MOOD ADJUSTERS
Psalm 102

17 He will listen to the prayers of the destitute, for He is never too busy to heed their requests.

Psalm 147

1 Hallelujah! Yes, praise the Lord! How good it is to sing His praises! How delightful, and how right!

3 He heals the brokenhearted, binding up their wounds.

4 He counts the stars and calls them all by name.

5 How great He is! His power is absolute! His understanding is unlimited.

MESSAGES TO THE BROKENHEARTED
Philippians 3

1 Whatever happens, dear friends, be glad in the Lord. I never get tired of telling you this and it is good for you to hear it again and again.

Psalm 31

24 So cheer up! Take courage if you are depending on the Lord.

Hosea 6

1 Come, let us return to the Lord; it is He who has torn us—He will heal us. He has wounded—He will bind us up.

2 In just a couple of days, or three at the most, He will set us on our feet again, to live in His kindness!

3 Oh, that we might know the Lord! Let us press on to know Him, and He will respond to us as surely as the coming of dawn or the rain of early spring.

HOPE AHEAD FOR YOU!
Psalm 43

5 O my soul, why be so gloomy and discouraged? Trust in God! I shall again praise Him for His wondrous help; He will make me smile again, *for He is my God!*

Isaiah 51

11 The time will come when God's redeemed will all come home again. They shall come with singing to Jerusalem, filled with joy and everlasting gladness; sorrow and mourning will all disappear.

12 I, even I, am He who comforts you and gives you all this joy.

2 Peter 3

13 But we are looking forward to God's promise of new heavens and a new earth afterwards, where there will be only goodness.

YET WILL I TRUST HIM!
Habakkuk 3

17 Even though the fig trees are all destroyed, and there is neither blossom left nor fruit, and though the olive crops all fail, and the fields lie barren; even if the flocks die in the fields and the cattle barns are empty,

18 Yet I will rejoice in the Lord; I will be happy in the God of my salvation.

19 The Lord God is my Strength, and He will give me the speed of a deer and bring me safely over the mountains.

13

When You Feel TEMPTED

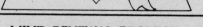

MIND RENEWAL PROMISE:
1 Corinthians 10

13b And no temptation is irresistible. You can trust God to keep the temptation from becoming so strong that you can't stand up against it, for He has promised this and will do what He says. He will show you how to escape temptation's power so that you can bear up patiently against it.

GOD UNDERSTANDS YOUR WEAKNESSES
Hebrews 4

14 But Jesus the Son of God is our great High Priest who has gone to heaven itself to help us; therefore let us never stop trusting Him.

15 This High Priest of ours understands our weaknesses, since He had the same temptations we do, though He never once gave way to them and sinned.

16 So let us come boldly to the very throne of God and stay there to receive His mercy and to find grace to help us in our times of need.

YOU ARE NOT ALONE IN TEMPTATION
1 Corinthians 10

13a But remember this—the wrong desires that

come into your life aren't anything new and different. Many others have faced exactly the same problems before you.

STRENGTH TO RESIST TEMPTATION
2 Thessalonians 3

2 Pray too that we will be saved out of the clutches of evil men, for not everyone loves the Lord.

3 But the Lord is faithful; He will make you strong and guard you from satanic attacks of every kind.

James 4

5 Or what do you think the Scripture means when it says that the Holy Spirit, whom God has placed within us, watches over us with tender jealousy?

6 But He gives us more and more strength to stand against all such evil longings.

SPECIAL PROMISES FOR OVERCOMERS
2 Peter 2

9 So also the Lord can rescue you and me from the temptations that surround us, and continue to punish the ungodly until the day of final judgment comes.

1 Corinthians 1

7 Now you have every grace and blessing; every spiritual gift and power for doing His will are yours during this time of waiting for the return of our Lord Jesus Christ.

INCENTIVE FOR OVERCOMERS
Psalm 19

7,8 God's laws are perfect. They protect us, make us wise, and give us joy and light.

9 God's laws are pure, eternal, just.

10 They are more desirable than gold. They are sweeter than honey dripping from a honeycomb.

11 For they warn us away from harm and give success to those who obey them.

Romans 14

10 You have no right to criticize your brother or look down on him. Remember, each of us will stand personally before the Judgment Seat of God.

11 For it is written, "As I live," says the Lord, "every knee shall bow to Me and every tongue confess to God."

12 Yes, each of us will give an account of himself to God.

REWARDS FOR OVERCOMING
Psalm 92

12 But the godly shall flourish like palm trees, and grow tall as the cedars of Lebanon.

13 For they are transplanted into the Lord's own garden, and are under His personal care.

14 Even in old age they will still produce fruit and be vital and green.

15 This honors the Lord, and exhibits His faithful care. He is my shelter. There is nothing but goodness in Him!

Matthew 5

8 Happy are those whose hearts are pure, for they shall see God.

Psalm 17

15 But as for me, my contentment is not in

wealth but in seeing You and knowing all is well between us. And when I awake in heaven, I will be fully satisfied, for I will see You face to face.

1 John 2

16 For all these worldly things, these evil desires—the craze for sex, the ambition to buy everything that appeals to you, and the pride that comes from wealth and importance—these are not from God. They are from this evil world itself.

17 And this world is fading away, and these evil, forbidden things will go with it, but whoever keeps doing the will of God will live forever.

28 And now, my little children, stay in happy fellowship with the Lord so that when He comes you will be sure that all is well, and will not have to be ashamed and shrink back from meeting Him.

PERFECT JUSTICE
1 Peter 1

17 And remember that your heavenly Father to whom you pray has no favorites when He judges. He will judge you with perfect justice for everything you do; so act in reverent fear of Him from now on until you get to heaven.

18 God paid a ransom to save you from the impossible road to heaven which your fathers tried to take, and the ransom He paid was not mere gold or silver, as you very well know.

19 But He paid for you with the precious life-blood of Christ, the sinless, spotless Lamb of God.

THERE IS REFUGE FOR THE BLAMELESS
Psalm 15

1 Lord, who may go and find refuge and shelter

in Your tabernacle up on Your holy hill?

2 Anyone who leads a blameless life and is truly sincere.

3 Anyone who refuses to slander others, does not listen to gossip, never harms his neighbor,

4 Speaks out against sin, criticizes those committing it, commends the faithful followers of the Lord, keeps a promise even if it ruins him,

5 Does not crush his debtors with high interest rates, and refuses to testify against the innocent despite the bribes offered him—such a man shall stand firm forever.

GOD'S ARMOR TO RESIST TEMPTATION
Ephesians 6

11 Put on all of God's armor so that you will be able to stand safe against all strategies and tricks of Satan.

12 For we are not fighting against people made of flesh and blood, but against persons without bodies—the evil rulers of the unseen world, those mighty satanic beings and great evil princes of darkness who rule this world; and against huge numbers of wicked spirits in the spirit world.

13 So use every piece of God's armor to resist the enemy whenever he attacks, and when it is all over, you will still be standing up.

14 But to do this, you will need the strong belt of truth and the breastplate of God's approval.

15 Wear shoes that are able to speed you on as you preach the Good News of peace with God.

16 In every battle you will need faith as your shield to stop the fiery arrows aimed at you by Satan.

17 And you will need the helmet of salvation and the sword of the Spirit—which is the Word of God.

18 Pray all the time. Ask God for anything in line with the Holy Spirit's wishes. Plead with Him, reminding Him of your needs, and keep praying earnestly for all Christians everywhere.

ADVICE
Psalm 32

8 I will instruct you (says the Lord) and guide you along the best pathway for your life; I will advise you and watch your progress.

9 Don't be like a senseless horse or mule that has to have a bit in its mouth to keep it in line!

MORE ADVICE: PRAY!
Matthew 26

41 Keep alert and pray. Otherwise temptation will overpower you. For the spirit indeed is willing, but how weak the body is!

Galatians 5

16 I advise you to obey only the Holy Spirit's instructions. He will tell you where to go and what to do, and then you won't always be doing the wrong things your evil nature wants you to.

17 For we naturally love to do evil things that are just the opposite from the things that the Holy Spirit tells us to do; and the good things we want to do when the Spirit has His way with us are just the opposite of our natural desires. These two forces within us are constantly fighting each other to win control over us, and our wishes are never free from their pressures.

Matthew 6

9 Pray along these lines: Our Father in heaven, we honor Your holy name.

10 We ask that Your kingdom will come now. May Your will be done here on earth, just as it is in heaven.

13 Don't bring us into temptation, but deliver us from the Evil One. Amen.

HELP FROM SLIPPING BACK
Jude

24,25 And now—all glory to Him who alone is God, who saves us through Jesus Christ our Lord; yes, splendor and majesty, all power and authority are His from the beginning; His they are and His they evermore shall be. And He is able to keep you from slipping and falling away, and to bring you, sinless and perfect, into His glorious presence with mighty shouts of everlasting joy. Amen.

BIBLE HELP FOR RESISTING TEMPTATION
Deuteronomy 17

18 And when he has been crowned and sits upon his throne as king, then he must copy these laws from the book kept by the Levite-priests.

19 That copy of the laws shall be his constant companion. He must read from it every day of his life so that he will learn to respect the Lord his God by obeying all of His commands.

20 This regular reading of God's laws will prevent him from feeling that he is better than his fellow citizens. It will also prevent him from turning away from God's laws in the slightest respect.

PRAYER FOR THE TIME YOU DO STUMBLE AND FALL BACK
Psalm 19

13 And keep me from deliberate wrongs; help me to stop doing them. Only then can I be free of guilt and innocent of some great crime.

14 May my spoken words and unspoken thoughts be pleasing even to You, O Lord my Rock and my Redeemer.

When You Feel
UNLOVED

MIND RENEWAL PROMISE:
Ephesians 3

17b ...May your roots go down deep into the soil of God's marvelous love;

18,19 and may you be able to feel and understand, as all God's children should, how long, how wide, how deep, and how high His love really is; and to experience this love for yourselves, though it is so great that you will never see the end of it or fully know or understand it. And so at last you will be filled up with God Himself.

SEE HOW GOD LOVES YOU!
Isaiah 46

3b ...I have created you and cared for you since you were born.

4 I will be your God through all your lifetime, yes, even when your hair is white with age. I made you and I will care for you. I will carry you along and be your Savior.

GOD'S LOVE PROVED
1 John 4

10 In this act we see what real love is: it is not

our love for God, but His love for us when He sent His Son to satisfy God's anger against our sins.

16 We know how much God loves us because we have felt His love and because we believe Him when He tells us that He loves us dearly. God is love, and anyone who lives in love is living with God and God is living in him.

18 We need have no fear of someone who loves us perfectly; His perfect love for us eliminates all dread of what He might do to us. If we are afraid, it is for fear of what He might do to us, and shows that we are not fully convinced that He really loves us.

19 So you see, our love for Him comes as a result of His loving us first.

DEEP LOVE
1 Corinthians 2

9b ...No mere man has ever seen, heard or even imagined what wonderful things God has ready for those who love the Lord.

Isaiah 40

11 He will feed his flock like a shepherd; He will carry the lambs in His arms and gently lead the ewes with young.

DEEP CONCERN
Psalm 139

13 You made all the delicate, inner parts of my body, and knit them together in my mother's womb.

14 Thank you for making me so wonderfully complex! It is amazing to think about. Your workmanship is marvelous—and how well I know it.

15 You were there while I was being formed in utter seclusion!

16 You saw me before I was born and scheduled each day of my life before I began to breathe. Every day was recorded in Your book!

Matthew 10

29 Not one sparrow (What do they cost? Two for a penny?) can fall to the ground without your Father knowing it.

30 And the very hairs of your head are all numbered.

31 So don't worry! You are more valuable to Him than many sparrows.

DEEP COMPASSION
Psalm 27

10 ...If my father and mother should abandon me, You would welcome and comfort me.

LOOK! THIS IS HOW GOD VIEWS YOU:
1 John 3

1 See how very much our heavenly Father loves us, for He allows us to be called His children—think of it—and we really *are*! But since most people don't know God, naturally they don't understand that we are His children.

2 Yes, dear friends, we are already God's children, right now, and we can't even imagine what it is going to be like later on.

A SPECIAL GIFT TO GOD
Ephesians 1

11 Moreover, because of what Christ has done we have become gifts to God that He delights in, for as part of God's sovereign plan we were chosen from the beginning to be His.

GOD REJOICES OVER YOU!
Zephaniah 3

17,18 For the Lord your God has arrived to live among you. He is a mighty Savior. He will give you victory. He will rejoice over you in great gladness; He will love you and not accuse you. Is that a joyous choir I hear? No, it is the Lord Himself exulting over you in happy song.

NEVER FAILING LOVE
Psalm 31

20 Hide your loved ones in the shelter of Your presence, safe beneath Your hand, safe from all conspiring men.

21 Blessed is the Lord, for He has shown me that His never-failing love protects me like the walls of a fort!

POWERFUL THOUGHTS
John 16

27 The Father Himself loves you dearly because you love Me and believe that I came from the Father.

Romans 5

8 But God showed His great love for us by sending Christ to die for us while we were still sinners.

Revelation 1

5b ...All praise to Him who always loves us and who set us free from our sins by pouring out His lifeblood for us.

15

When You Feel
WEAK, INCAPABLE

MIND RENEWAL PROMISE:
Philippians 4

13 For I can do everything God asks me to with the help of Christ who gives the strength and power.

"MY POWER SHOWS BEST
IN WEAK PEOPLE"—God

2 Corinthians 12

8 Three different times I begged God to make me well again.

9 Each time He said, "No. But I am with you; that is all you need. My power shows up best in weak people." Now I am glad to boast about how weak I am; I am glad to be a living demonstration of Christ's power, instead of showing off my own power and abilities.

10 Since I know it is all for Christ's good, I am quite happy about "the thorn," and about insults and hardships, persecutions and difficulties; for when I am weak, then I am strong—the less I have, the more I depend on Him.

PRAY FOR GOD'S STRENGTH—YOU WILL GET IT THEN

Mark 11

22,23 In reply Jesus said to the disciples, "If you only have faith in God—this is the absolute truth—you can say to this Mount of Olives, 'Rise up and fall into the Mediterranean,' and your command will be obeyed. All that's required is that you really believe and have no doubt!

24 Listen to Me! You can pray for *anything*, and *if you believe, you have it*; it's yours!"

2 Chronicles 16

9 For the eyes of the Lord search back and forth across the whole earth, looking for people whose hearts are perfect toward Him, so that He can show His great power in helping them.

NO WEAKNESS HERE!!
2 Corinthians 13

3b ...Christ is not weak in His dealings with you, but is a mighty power within you.

4 His weak, human body died on the cross, but now He lives by the mighty power of God. We, too, are weak in our bodies, as He was, but now we live and are strong, as He is, and have all of God's power to use.

STRONG PROMISES FOR WEAK PEOPLE
2 Timothy 2

13 Even when we are too weak to have any faith left, He remains faithful to us and will help us, for He cannot disown us who are part of Himself, and He will always carry out His promises to us.

Zechariah 10

12 The Lord says, "I will make My people strong with power from Me! They will go wherever they wish, and wherever they go, they will be under My personal care."

SPECIAL STRENGTH FOR THE WEARY
Isaiah 40

28 Don't you yet understand? Don't you know by now that the everlasting God, the Creator of the farthest parts of the earth, never grows faint or weary? No one can fathom the depths of His understanding.

29 He gives power to the tired and worn out, and strength to the weak.

Luke 18

27 He replied, "God can do what men can't!"

MEET YOUR HELPER
Psalm 89

7 The highest of angelic powers stand in dread and awe of Him. Who is as revered as He by those surrounding Him?

8 O Jehovah, Commander of the heavenly armies, where is there any other Mighty One like You? Faithfulness is Your very character.

9 You rule the oceans when their waves arise in fearful storms; You speak, and they lie still.

11 The heavens are Yours, the world, everything—for You created them all.

12 You created north and south! Mount Tabor and Mount Hermon rejoice to be signed by Your name as their maker!

13 Strong is Your arm! Strong is Your hand!
Your right hand is lifted high in glorious strength.

MEET ONE WHO WAS HELPED
Psalm 94

16 Who will protect me from the wicked? Who
will be my shield?

17 I would have died unless the Lord had
helped me.

18 I screamed, "I'm slipping, Lord!" and He
was kind and saved me.

HOW TO BE "UP" IN A "DOWN" WORLD
Psalm 18

29 Now in Your strength I can scale any wall,
attack any troop.

30 What a God He is! How perfect in every
way! All His promises prove true. He is a shield
for everyone who hides behind Him.

31 For who is God except our Lord? Who but
He is as a rock?

32 He fills me with strength and protects me
wherever I go.

33 He gives me the surefootedness of a
mountain goat upon the crags. He leads me safely
along the top of the cliffs.

Zechariah 4

6b ....Not by might, nor by power, but by My
Spirit, says the Lord of Hosts—you will succeed
because of My Spirit, though you are few and
weak.

CHILDREN OF GOD, STOP CRINGING!!
Romans 8

14 For all who are led by the Spirit of God are sons of God.

15 And so we should not be like cringing, fearful slaves, but we should behave like God's very own children, adopted into the bosom of His family, and calling to Him, "Father, Father."

Ephesians 1

19 I pray that you will begin to understand how incredibly great His power is to help those who believe Him. It is that same mighty power

20 That raised Christ from the dead and seated Him in the place of honor at God's right hand in heaven.

THE BATTLE IS GOD'S, NOT YOURS
2 Chronicles 20

15b ... The Lord says, "Don't be afraid! Don't be paralyzed by this mighty army! For the battle is not yours, but God's!"

POWER FOR SUPERNATURAL LIVING
Ephesians 3

20 Now glory be to God who by His mighty power at work within us is able to do far more than we would ever dare to ask or even dream of—infinitely beyond our highest prayers, desires, thoughts, or hopes.

2 Samuel 22

29 O Lord, You are my light! You make my darkness bright!

30 By Your power I can crush an army; by Your strength I leap over a wall.

33 God is my strong fortress; He has made me safe.

34 He causes the good to walk a steady tread like mountain goats upon the rocks.

37 You have made wide steps for my feet, to keep them from slipping.

50 No wonder I give thanks to You, O Lord, among the nations; and sing praises to Your name.

MORE POWER TO YOU!!
Psalm 91

13 You can safely meet a lion or step on poisonous snakes, yes, even trample them beneath your feet!

14 For the Lord says, "Because he loves Me, I will rescue him; I will make him great because he trusts in My name.

15 When he calls on Me I will answer; I will be with him in trouble, and rescue him and honor him."

2 Corinthians 4

16 That is why we never give up. Though our bodies are dying, our inner strength in the Lord is growing every day.

Jeremiah 32

27 I am the Lord, the God of all mankind; is there anything too hard for Me?

Isaiah 64

1 Oh, that You would burst forth from the skies and come down! How the mountains would quake in Your presence!

2 The consuming fire of Your glory would burn down the forests and boil the oceans dry. The nations would tremble before You; then Your enemies would learn the reason for Your fame!

3 So it was before when You came down, for You did awesome things beyond our highest expectations, and how the mountains quaked!

4 For since the world began no one has seen or heard of such a God as ours, who works for those who wait for Him!

16

When You Feel WORTHLESS, INSIGNIFICANT

MIND RENEWAL PROMISE:
1 Samuel 16

7 But the Lord said to Samuel, "Don't judge by a man's face or height, for this is not the one. I don't make decisions the way you do! Men judge by outward appearance, but I look at a man's thoughts and intentions."

WHO IS A WORTHLESS PERSON?
Proverbs 6

12,13 Let me describe for you a worthless and a wicked man; first he is a constant liar; he signals his true intentions to his friends with eyes and feet and fingers.

14 Next, his heart is full of rebellion. And he spends his time thinking of all the evil he can do, and stirring up discontent.

15 But he will be destroyed suddenly, broken beyond hope of healing.

16-19 For there are six things the Lord hates—no, seven; haughtiness, lying, murdering, plotting evil, eagerness to do wrong, a false witness, sowing discord among brothers.

Jeremiah 17

5 The Lord says: Cursed is the man who puts his trust in mortal man and turns his heart away from God.

6 He is like a stunted shrub in the desert, with no hope for the future; he lives on the salt-encrusted plains in the barren wilderness; good times pass him by forever.

WHAT MAKES A PERSON WORTHWHILE IN GOD'S SIGHT?

People who acknowledge God are worthwhile:
Luke 12

8 And I assure you of this: I, the Messiah, will publicly honor you in the presence of God's angels if you publicly acknowledge Me here on earth as your Friend.

Humble people are worthwhile:
Luke 14

11 For everyone who tries to honor himself shall be humbled; and he who humbles himself shall be honored.

People who serve others are worthwhile:
Matthew 23

11 The more lowly your service to others, the greater you are. To be the greatest, be a servant.

12 But those who think themselves great shall be disappointed and humbled; and those who humble themselves shall be exalted.

People who want to obey God are worthwhile:
John 14

21 The one who obeys Me is the one who loves

Me; and because he loves Me, My Father will love him; and I will too, and I will reveal Myself to him.

People who trust God are worthwhile:
Jeremiah 17

7 But blessed is the man who trusts in the Lord and has made the Lord his hope and confidence.

8 He is like a tree planted along a riverbank, with its roots reaching deep into the water—a tree not bothered by the heat nor worried by long months of drought. Its leaves stay green and it goes right on producing all its luscious fruit.

The ultimate trait (check yourself)
1 Corinthians 13

1 If I had the gift of being able to speak in other languages without learning them, and could speak in every language there is in all of heaven and earth, but didn't love others, I would only be making noise.

2 If I had the gift of prophecy and knew all about what is going to happen in the future, knew everything about *everything*, but didn't love others, what good would it do? Even If I had the gift of faith so that I could speak to a mountain and make it move, I would still be worth nothing at all without love.

4 Love is very patient and kind, never jealous or envious, never boastful or proud,

5 Never haughty or selfish or rude. Love does not demand its own way. It is not irritable or touchy. It does not hold grudges and will hardly even notice when others do it wrong.

6 It is never glad about injustice, but rejoices whenever truth wins out.

7 If you love someone you will be loyal to him no matter what the cost. You will always believe in him, always expect the best of him, and always stand your ground in defending him.

8 All the special gifts and powers from God will some day come to an end, but love goes on forever.

CAUTION!!
Romans 12

3 As God's messenger I give each of you God's warning: Be honest in your estimate of yourselves, measuring your value by how much faith God has given you.

YOU ARE A DIVINELY UNIQUE PERSON
1 Corinthians 12

1 And now, brothers, I want to write about the special abilities the Holy Spirit gives to each of you, for I don't want any misunderstanding about them.

4 Now God gives us many kinds of special abilities, but it is the same Holy Spirit who is the source of them all.

5 There are different kinds of service to God, but it is the same Lord we are serving.

6 There are many ways in which God works in our lives, but it is the same God who does the work in and through all of us who are His.

7 The Holy Spirit displays God's power through each of us as a means of helping the entire church.

8 To one person the Spirit gives the ability to give wise advice; someone else may be especially good at studying and teaching, and this is his gift from the same Spirit.

9 He gives special faith to another, and to someone else the power to heal the sick.

10 He gives power for doing miracles to some, and to others power to prophesy and preach. He gives someone else the power to know whether evil spirits are speaking through those who claim to be giving God's messages—or whether it is really the Spirit of God who is speaking. Still another person is able to speak in languages he never learned; and others, who do not know the language either, are given power to understand what he is saying.

YOU HAVE ABILITY TO DO CERTAIN THINGS WELL
Romans 12

4,5 Just as there are many parts to our bodies, so it is with Christ's body. We are all parts of it, and it takes every one of us to make it complete, for we each have different work to do. So we belong to each other, and each needs all the others.

6 God has given each of us the ability to do certain things well.

WEALTH DOES NOT MAKE YOU VALUABLE
Proverbs 22

2 The rich and the poor are alike before the Lord who made them all.

James 1

10,11 But a rich man should be glad that his riches mean nothing to the Lord, for he will soon be gone, like a flower that has lost its beauty and fades away, withered—killed by the scorching summer sun.

YOUR RACE, EDUCATION OR SOCIAL POSITION DO NOT MAKE YOU VALUABLE
Colossians 3

10 You are living a brand new kind of life that is continually learning more and more of what is right, and trying constantly to be more and more like Christ who created this new life within you.

11 In this new life one's nationality or race or education or social position is unimportant; such things mean nothing. Whether a person has Christ is what matters, and He is equally available to all.

CHRIST IN YOU—*THAT* MAKES YOU VALUABLE!
Hebrews 3

6 But Christ, God's faithful Son, is in complete charge of God's house. And we Christians are God's house—He lives in us!

2 Corinthians 2

15 As far as God is concerned there is a sweet, wholesome fragrance in our lives. It is the fragrance of Christ within us, an aroma to both the saved and the unsaved all around us.

Ephesians 1

18 I pray that your hearts will be flooded with light so that you can see something of the future He has called you to share. I want you to realize that God has been made rich because we who are Christ's have been given to Him!

PEOPLE IN THE BIBLE FELT
INFERIOR TOO
(Note how God took care of their inadequacy)

Moses
Exodus 4

1 But Moses said, "They won't believe me! They won't do what *I* tell them to. They'll say, 'Jehovah never appeared to you!'"

10 Moses pleaded, "O Lord, I'm just not a good speaker. I never have been, and I'm not now, even after You have spoken to me, for I have a speech impediment."

11 "Who makes mouths?" Jehovah asked him. "Isn't it I, the Lord? Who makes a man so that he can speak or not speak, see or not see, hear or not hear?

12 Now go ahead and do as I tell you, for I will help you to speak well, and I will tell you what to say."

13 But Moses said, "Lord, please! Send someone else."

14 Then the Lord became angry. "All right," He said, "your brother Aaron is a good speaker. And he is coming here to look for you, and will be very happy when he finds you.

15 So I will tell you what to tell him, and I will help both of you to speak well, and I will tell you what to do.

16 He will be your spokesman to the people. And you will be as God to him, telling him what to say..."

Jeremiah
Jeremiah 1

4,5 The Lord said to me, "I knew you before

you were formed within your mother's womb; before you were born I sanctified you and appointed you as my spokesman to the world."

6 "O Lord God," I said. "I can't do that! I'm far too young! I'm only a youth!"

7 "Don't say that," He replied, "for you will go wherever I send you and speak whatever I tell you to.

8 And don't be afraid of the people, for I, the Lord, will be with you and see you through."

9 Then He touched my mouth and said, "See, I have put My words in your mouth!"

Solomon
1 Kings 3

7 "O Lord my God, now you have made me the king instead of my father David, but I am as a little child who doesn't know his way around.

8 And here I am among Your own chosen people, a nation so great that there are almost too many people to count!

9 Give me an understanding mind so that I can govern Your people well and know the difference between what is right and what is wrong. For who by himself is able to carry such a heavy responsibility?"

10 The Lord was pleased with his reply and was glad that Solomon had asked for wisdom.

11 So He replied, "Because you have asked for wisdom in governing My people, and haven't asked for a long life or riches for yourself, or the defeat of your enemies—

12 Yes, I'll give you what you asked for! I will give you a wiser mind than anyone else has ever had or ever will have!

13 And I will also give you what you didn't ask for—riches and honor! And no one in all the world will be as rich and famous as you for the rest of your life!"

YOU ARE WORTH DYING FOR
2 Corinthians 5

15 He died for all.

16 So stop evaluating Christians by what the world thinks about them or by what they seem to be like on the outside.

Ephesians 2

4 But God is so rich in mercy; He loved us so much

5 That even though we were spiritually dead and doomed by our sins, He gave us back our lives again when He raised Christ from the dead—only by His undeserved favor have we ever been saved—

6 And lifted us up from the grave into glory along with Christ, where we sit with Him in the heavenly realms—all because of what Christ Jesus did.

POWERFUL THOUGHT
1 Corinthians 1

26 Notice among ourselves, dear brothers, that few of us who follow Christ have big names or power or wealth.

27 Instead, God has deliberately chosen to save those whom the world considers foolish and of little worth in order to shame those the world considers wise and great.

28 He has chosen the little people, those despised by the world, who just don't count for

anything at all, and used them to bring down to nothing those the world considers great.

30 For it is from God alone that you have your life through Jesus Christ. He showed us God's plan of salvation; He was the one who made us acceptable to God; He made us pure and holy and gave Himself to purchase our salvation.

31 As it says in the Scriptures, "If anyone is going to boast, let him only boast of what the Lord has done."

Have You Heard of the

Four Spiritual Laws?

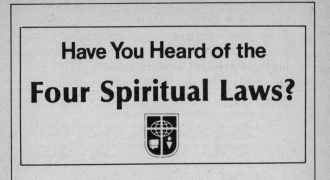

1

Just as there are physical laws that govern the physical universe, so are there spiritual laws which govern your relationship with God.

LAW ONE

GOD **LOVES** YOU, AND OFFERS A WONDERFUL **PLAN** FOR YOUR LIFE.

(References contained in this booklet should be read in context from the Bible wherever possible.)

God's Love

"For God so loved the world, that He gave His only begotten Son, that whoever believes in Him should not perish, but have eternal life" (John 3:16).

God's Plan

(Christ speaking) "I came that they might have life, and might have it abundantly" (that it might be full and meaningful) (John 10:10).

Why is it that most people are not experiencing the abundant life? Because . . .

LAW TWO

MAN IS **SINFUL** AND **SEPARATED** FROM GOD. THEREFORE, HE CANNOT KNOW AND EXPERIENCE GOD'S LOVE AND PLAN FOR HIS LIFE.

Man Is Sinful

"For all have sinned and fall short of the glory of God" (Romans 3:23).

Man was created to have fellowship with God; but, because of his stubborn self-will, he chose to go his own independent way and fellowship with God was broken. This self-will, characterized by an attitude of active rebellion or passive indifference, is evidence of what the Bible calls sin.

Man Is Separated

"For the wages of sin is death" (spiritual separation from God) (Romans 6:23).

HOLY GOD

SINFUL MAN

This diagram illustrates that God is holy and man is sinful. A great gulf separates the two. The arrows illustrate that man is continually trying to reach God and the abundant life through his own efforts, such as a good life, philosophy or religion.

The third law explains the only way to bridge this gulf . . .

LAW THREE

JESUS CHRIST IS GOD'S **ONLY** PROVISION FOR MAN'S SIN. THROUGH HIM YOU CAN KNOW AND EXPERIENCE GOD'S LOVE AND PLAN FOR YOUR LIFE.

He Died in Our Place

"But God demonstrates His own love toward us, in that while we were yet sinners, Christ died for us" (Romans 5:8).

He Rose from the Dead

"Christ died for our sins . . . He was buried . . . He was raised on the third day, according to the Scriptures . . . He appeared to Peter, then to the twelve. After that He appeared to more than five hundred . . ." (I Corinthians 15:3-6).

He Is the Only Way to God

"Jesus said to him, 'I am the way, and the truth, and the life; no one comes to the Father, but through Me' " (John 14:6).

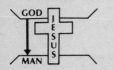

This diagram illustrates that God has bridged the gulf which separates us from Him by sending His Son, Jesus Christ, to die on the cross in our place to pay the penalty for our sins.

It is not enough just to know these three laws . . .

4 LAW FOUR

WE MUST INDIVIDUALLY **RECEIVE** JESUS CHRIST AS SAVIOR AND LORD; THEN WE CAN KNOW AND EXPERIENCE GOD'S LOVE AND PLAN FOR OUR LIVES.

We Must Receive Christ

"But as many as received Him, to them He gave the right to become children of God, even to those who believe in His name" (John 1:12).

We Receive Christ Through Faith

"For by grace you have been saved through faith; and that not of yourselves, it is the gift of God; not as a result of works, that no one should boast" (Ephesians 2:8,9).

When We Receive Christ, We Experience a New Birth.
(Read John 3:1-8.)

We Receive Christ by Personal Invitation

(Christ is speaking): "Behold, I stand at the door and knock; if any one hears My voice and opens the door, I will come in to him" (Revelation 3:20).

Receiving Christ involves turning to God from self (repentance) and trusting Christ to come into our lives to forgive our sins and to make us the kind of people He wants us to be. Just to agree intellectually that Jesus Christ is the Son of God and that He died on the cross for our sins is not enough. Nor is it enough to have an emotional experience. We receive Jesus Christ by faith, as an act of the will.

These two circles represent two kinds of lives:

SELF-DIRECTED LIFE
S — Self is on the throne
† — Christ is outside the life
● — Interests are directed by self, often resulting in discord and frustration

CHRIST-DIRECTED LIFE
† — Christ is in the life and on the throne
S — Self is yielding to Christ
● — Interests are directed by Christ, resulting in harmony with God's plan

Which circle best represents your life?
Which circle would you like to have represent your life?

The following explains how you can receive Christ:

YOU CAN RECEIVE CHRIST RIGHT NOW BY FAITH THROUGH PRAYER

(Prayer is talking with God)

God knows your heart and is not so concerned with your words as He is with the attitude of your heart. The following is a suggested prayer:

"Lord Jesus, I need You. Thank You for dying on the cross for my sins. I open the door of my life and receive You as my Savior and Lord. Thank You for forgiving my sins and giving me eternal life. Take control of the throne of my life. Make me the kind of person You want me to be."

Does this prayer express the desire of your heart?

If it does, pray this prayer right now, and Christ will come into your life, as He promised. .

How to Know That Christ Is in Your Life

Did you receive Christ into your life? According to His promise in Revelation 3:20, where is Christ right now in relation to you? Christ said that He would come into your life. Would He mislead you? On what authority do you know that God has answered your prayer? (The trustworthiness of God Himself and His Word.)

The Bible Promises Eternal Life to All Who Receive Christ

"And the witness is this, that God has given us eternal life, and this life is in His Son. He who has the Son has the life; he who does not have the Son of God does not have the life. These things I have written to you who believe in the name of the Son of God, in order that you may know that you have eternal life" (I John 5:11-13).

Thank God often that Christ is in your life and that He will never leave you (Hebrews 13:5). You can know on the basis of His promise that Christ lives in you and that you have eternal life, from the very moment you invite Him in. He will not deceive you.

An important reminder . . .

DO NOT DEPEND UPON FEELINGS

The promise of God's Word, the Bible — not our feelings — is our authority. The Christian lives by faith (trust) in the trustworthiness of God Himself and His Word. This train diagram illustrates the relationship between **fact** (God and His Word), **faith** (our trust in God and His Word), and **feeling** (the result of our faith and obedience) (John 14:21).

The train will run with or without the caboose. However, it would be useless to attempt to pull the train by the caboose. In the same way, we, as Christians, do not depend on feelings or emotions, but we place our faith (trust) in the trustworthiness of God and the promises of His Word.

NOW THAT YOU HAVE RECEIVED CHRIST

The moment that you received Christ by faith, as an act of the will, many things happened, including the following:

1. Christ came into your life (Revelation 3:20 and Colossians 1:27).
2. Your sins were forgiven (Colossians 1:14).
3. You became a child of God (John 1:12).
4. You received eternal life (John 5:24).
5. You began the great adventure for which God created you (John 10:10; II Corinthians 5:17 and I Thessalonians 5:18).

Can you think of anything more wonderful that could happen to you than receiving Christ? Would you like to thank God in prayer right now for what He has done for you? By thanking God, you demonstrate your faith.

To enjoy your new life
to the fullest . . .

SUGGESTIONS FOR CHRISTIAN GROWTH

Spiritual growth results from trusting Jesus Christ. "The righteous man shall live by faith" (Galatians 3:11). A life of faith will enable you to trust God increasingly with every detail of your life, and to practice the following:

G Go to God in prayer daily (John 15:7).

R Read God's Word daily (Acts 17:11)—begin with the Gospel of John.

O Obey God moment by moment (John 14:21).

W Witness for Christ by your life and words (Matthew 4:19; John 15:8).

T Trust God for every detail of your life (I Peter 5:7).

H Holy Spirit—allow Him to control and empower your daily life and witness (Galatians 5:16,17; Acts 1:8).

FELLOWSHIP IN A GOOD CHURCH

God's Word admonishes us not to forsake "the assembling of ourselves together. . ." (Hebrews 10:25). Several logs burn brightly together; but put one aside on the cold hearth and the fire goes out. So it is with your relationship to other Christians. If you do not belong to a church, do not wait to be invited. Take the initiative; call the pastor of a nearby church where Christ is honored and His Word is preached. Start this week, and make plans to attend regularly.

SPECIAL MATERIALS ARE AVAILABLE FOR CHRISTIAN GROWTH.

If you have come to know Christ personally through this presentation of the gospel, write for a free booklet especially written to assist you in your Christian growth.

A special Bible study series and an abundance of other helpful materials for Christian growth are also available. For additional information, please write Campus Crusade for Christ International, San Bernardino, CA 92414.

You will want to share this important discovery . . .

BENEDICTION
2 Thessalonians 2

16   May our Lord Jesus Christ Himself and God our Father, who has loved us and given us everlasting comfort and hope which we don't deserve,

17   Comfort your hearts with all comfort, and help you in every good thing you say and do.